DHARMA:

**Survey Of Indian Cultural Religion And
Spirituality Seen Through Brahmanic Eyes**

DHARMA:

Survey Of Indian Cultural Religion And
Spirituality Seen Through Brahmanic Eyes

DHARMA:

Survey Of Indian Cultural Religion And Spirituality Seen Through Brahmanic Eyes

by
Uma Marina Vesci

PILGRIMS PUBLISHING
◆ Varanasi ◆

DHARMA: Survey Of Indian Cultural Religion And Spirituality Seen Through Brahmanic Eyes
Uma Marina Vesci

Published by:
PILGRIMS PUBLISHING

An imprint of:
PILGRIMS BOOK HOUSE
(Distributors in India)
B 27/98 A-8, Nawabganj Road
Durga Kund, Varanasi-221010, India
Tel: 91-542- 2314060, 2312456
E-mail: pilgrims@satyam.net.in
Website: www.pilgrimsbooks.com

PILGRIMS BOOK HOUSE (New Delhi)
9 Netaji Subhash Marg, 2nd Floor
Near Neeru Hotel, Daryaganj, New Delhi 110002
Tel: 91-11-23285081 Fax: 91-11-23285722
E-mail: pilgrim@del2.vsnl.net.in

Distributed in Nepal by:
PILGRIMS BOOK HOUSE
P O Box 3872, Thamel, Kathmandu, Nepal
Tel: 977-1-4700942, Off: 977-1-4700919
Fax: 977-1-4700943
E-mail: pilgrims@wlink.com.np

First Edition
Copyright © 2005, Uma Marina Vesci
All Rights Reserved

Layout & Cover design by Asha Mishra

ISBN: 81-7769-270-4

Printed in India at Pilgrim Press Pvt. Ltd. Lalpur Varanasi

Contents

PREFACE

My aim in presenting a work of this vastness and magnitude is to be able to condense into a nutshell all the poignant features of a cultural world, which, for being so multifarious, variously articulated and, at first sight at least, so dispersed in thousands or millions of rivulets, can seldom be grasped in its totality. The task is full of risks, obviously, because, in order to be able to enlarge its panorama so as to include as many items as possible, one has to rise higher and higher (to borrow the image from an helicopter standard) thus missing any hope of proper detail. If, during the exposition from such a large scale perspective, for the sake of clarity or exemplification, some details attract more attention than others that does not mean that we alter our bird's-eye-view panorama but only that some areas in it would stick out as if pointed at by a large telescope.

The disadvantage of such a presentation is obviously the loss of depth, of the particular, with all its implications so that full justice cannot be expected. For knowing Indian culture in depth one has to break it down into its many segmentations and pick them up, one at a time, for further studies and understanding. This is the work of monographies, a few of whose have been quoted in a necessarily incomplete bibliography. Depth cannot go together with broadness, as any excavator of wells will confirm. The advantages, however, have been important enough to foster the present attempt. Viewing everything together brings out connections that are usually missed and may lead to discover an underlying unity between all the various strata, levels, idiosyncrasies and different types of kingdoms, historical periods, geographical areas and socio-religious features, which taken in isolation would appear antithetical to one another. An example could be the central position in forging the religious and cultural parameters and patterns assumed by the generally neglected Brahmanas (the exegetical portion of Vedic Sacred Scriptures). It is because of them that an almost forgotten past (the one chanted by the Ancient Rishis) has been recovered and moulded so as to suit a completely different contemporary situation in order, at its turn, to be hurled into the future...a future still alive today after thousands of years. Or, to take another instance, one is made aware of a loose equivalence between the two major Gods of the two major Pantheons raised to prominence in the popular, or exoteric, Hindu religion, yet complementary in their respective differences.

Now, with the purpose of still widening a possible field of eventual comparisons, say with other religions or spiritualities—a task rather urgent in a modern world where people of all races and standards are thrown together by a large-scale peaceful migrations—it is not perhaps useless to preface this view of Brahmanism with a global view: that of the various religions of the world. There are almost an unlimited number of them but, if arranged in a proper historical pattern, one may be able to perceive that, after all, they can be put into some convenient and intelligible groups, amounting in all, in my opinion, to five, making comparisons if not easier at least more feasible.

These five groups may be presented in a very schematic manner, taking into consideration, as leading marks for the division, their socio-historical situations regardless of their specific contents, which in any case, notwithstanding the immense inner differentiations, also can automatically follow into their allotted place in the pattern, though presenting wide theoretical differences in their theological contents.

1. The first group consists of all those religions that by scholars dealing with them have been classified as "primitive", or "pre-historic" or "ethnic" or "tribal". They are those forms of culture and spiritualities that have grown together with the people responsible for them. They normally deal with the 'histories', socio-political, ritual behaviour of their own 'tribes' within the boundaries of a given, generally small, society and establish or regulate their relationship within themselves and with a Superior Power. The number of these religions, or if preferred: of local spiritualities, is virtually beyond counting since they range from earliest pre-history of mankind down to the ethnological populations still alive today. Since their influence does not spread much outside the geographical limits of a single folk generally not exceeding an area of few villages inhabited by a rather small and manageable quantity of families and individuals, one can easily surmise the almost infinite quantity of them. But however great the disparity in time, space and content, all of them can be clustered together in so far as they share certain characteristics—such as: comparatively small and compact societies, a roughly similar conception of the Divine seen more as an indefinite Power then a personal Deity, and also a somehow

homologable set of ritual and cultural behaviour. Since such religions are usually self-sufficient and tend to close on themselves, for a long time they remained outside the awareness of other people, so that, when finally 'discovered' by the inquisitive minds of the Westerners, they were at first considered "primitive" or not rising above a rather simplistic side. Now, however, since more people are approaching these worlds with a more genuine desire not only to understand them in a deeper way, but also to participate in their beliefs and cultural behaviours, their great spiritual depth is getting a better recognition at a great rate.

2. Properly speaking, this second group hosts what can be considered "religions" in the more appropriate sense of the word. They are made of all that is regarded as pertinent to religion as such: proper personal Deities with well defined characters and proper myths delineating their genesis and activities, and interrelated among themselves in well constructed Pantheons; a well established and structured cult, especially centred on Sacrifice as its main item, drawing to its pattern the activities of poets for producing the hymns to be recited along and that very important of the priests engaged in their performances; and beside, the presence of temples, statues for worship and other similar paraphernalia. In a word, only these religions can be considered to be regular Theims, or rather Polytheisms (since the only monotheism found at that early times was that of the Hebrews in so far as theirs was the protective God of a single tribe) and they are nationally built. This is to say that all these religions grew within and together with the people in the process of settling permanently in a given country and turning their way of life into a more stable, cultural and nationalistic frame. In this process of a totally new religious and cultural creation, the almost forgotten past could not be get rid off altogether, and was either tolerated as surviving popular forms or sublimated in a kind of 'lost paradise' where all perfections abided.

Needless to say that those Polytheisms were strictly bound to their respective nations (and vice-versa, of course), so that they were destroyed with the destruction of their worshippers in the same way as success in destroying their principal protecting Divinity was tantamount to have accomplished the conquest of the enemy. Since none of such ancient nations have survived with the same political standard that supported their related Pantheons, practically all of them have disappeared with the collapse of their related empires all, but for just a few exceptions. Such exceptions are found in those religions where, while still at their peak, a drastic change toward a spiritual interiorisation took place at the hand of one or a few 'enlighten souls' fighting the 'establishment'. That interiorisation, starting with a drive toward a reform into their main cult, sacrifice, ended up by disentangling the 'national' Divine Power from Its geographical hold, with the result that, when their respective nations actually collapsed under the impact of foreign invasions or inner turmoil's, such Divine could survive into a more universalised and spiritualised level. These religions belong to the 3rd group.

3. Such religions, as seen, are very limited since their number does not exceed the ciphers 5 or 6 and most of them got to that saving process of transformation and spiritualization more or less at the same historical period: between the VIIth and the VIth centuries BC. They are located, beginning from the East, two in China, then in India, Persia, and Israel. The latter was the first experiencing the soundness of its inner reform because that spiritualization enabled its God to survive the destruction of his Temple and this allowed his people to keep together and not to give up hope and faith even after the political collapse of their nation, first at the hand of the Babylonians in the middle of the VIth century BC and, then, even more drastically when this country was definitely destroyed by the Romans in the year 70 AD. Yahweh was above space and time, though not of racial ties, and the erasing of His earthly sacred place instead of spelling His doom rather strengthened His own power and influence on His people dispersed all over the world (in the Diaspora).

In China the spiritual reforms brought about by single figures like Confucius and Lao Tse enabled the nation to go through a good deal of political transformations, changes in ruling dynasties, and forceful invasions of other, still more universal, spiritualities and ideologies. Both these spiritual leaders acted inside the religious and cultural framework of their nation, Confucius even editing anew the ancient Sacred Texts of their ancient Past, but their turned their inner meaning into a high spiritual standard freeing it from earthly political ups and downs, but not from a broad cultural background, which was able to maintain such reforms solidly grasped in the Chinese roots and character.

In India, the Seers of the Upanishads, and, to an extent that had less bearing within its regions, by the heterodox Jains and Buddhists, as scanning the following pages could see it, brought about such spiritualising movement. The orthodox import of such attempts of interiorization and spiritualization can be noted in the change that occurred in the popular religiosity transmitted by the Epic and Puranic literatures (see below, in its proper place) and kept Hinduism alive even when the previous ways of life were superseded by new political orders and by the impact of the 'missionary' religions of the following group. As for the Heterodox groups, the Jains influence was restricted to a rather small group of people turning themselves into a caste, while the more disturbing Buddhism was finally expelled by the country and shall be found again in the next group.

A less imposing influence seems to have been attached to the Zoroastrian universalising reform of Avestic religion in Persia. Though its influence spread across its national boundaries into the Roman empire leaving substantial traces in the religion that took over after the latter political collapse, in its own country was superseded by the invasion of another spirituality (again belonging to the next group) and its followers were chased away and now they survive in a small ethnic group mostly located in the West part of India: the Parsi. Though forced to migrate elsewhere, this universalised religion did not follow the fate of those belonging to the next group, because it did not loose its cultural roots, not its basic nationalistic pattern.

The main common features in these otherwise very different spiritualities, is their streak of universalisation imposed to their national concept of the Divine, the disentangling of their figures from their cultic images and temples, the stress given to moral conduct and inner personal relationship with the ensuing spiritual God aiming at individual growth and salvation. Yet, all this remained strictly within the area of their respective 'national' religions, somehow incurring, at first, into superficial (though sometimes bitter) clashes with orthodox authorities, but to be later accepted and followed when petty concerns for personal advantages were finally overcome. Such inner movements had, therefore, a double advantage: to free the Divine from a too involving national situation (forerunner of its destruction) but at the same time saving ancestral roots, thus officially still retaining inner national and vital ties. The same thing did not happen to a second wave of interiorising move, occurring within the areas of Judaism and Hinduism, giving rise to a further group, the 4th in line.

4. This group is made by those, even fewer, religions, which did arise from a second attempt of deepening the previous spiritual reforms, but were not accepted by their own people. The result was that their believers were compelled to run away from their main land and to free themselves totally from any remnant and contact with their 'mother-land' or better 'parental-religion'. Such new religions, so uprooted from their nurturing cultural soil, are: Buddhism, a further radical movement from the Upanishads brought about by the forceful personality of Gautama the

Buddha and thrown out of its country when, after few centuries, Hinduism reintegrated what could be absorbed of its message and drastically rejected what was contrary to its structural pattern; Christianity, a further deepening of Prophetic universalisation within Judaism, preached by the Rabbi Jesus from Nazareth, the Christ, and rejected already at its start by Jewish authorities, just forcing it to find a different cultural soil where to spread its Founder's message of Salvation. Both of them, though absolutely different in content, share the common fate of having been born within a tradition which ejected them and so uprooted them from their proper cultural soil; both, then, had to find another ground for developing, a fact that bore immense consequences in their inner setting converting them into something more like to a Super-religion above national particularises but also a natural sense of 'belonging'. The third of the group is Islam, that also shares the same destiny, though with a reverse movement because in its case the Founder belonged to the 'receiving soil'. For the rest the case of this other Message of Salvation for the entire humanity was in the same position as the other two and with the same results. Islam, in fact, produced a drastic change in the Arabic national religion through a completely new experience inspired by the Jewish monotheistic God. In other words, Mohammad, though he an Arab, turned outside his country for parameters that he found more suitable to express his personal experience. The end results were, therefore, somehow on the same lines as those of the two previously mentioned Super-religions which brought new spiritual parameters on quite alien national traditions, involving in the process a drastic adaptation both in the salvific messages and in the receiving grounds.

The main import of such refusals by their mother-religions was a forced uprootedness befalling the three of them (including Islam through its acceptance of an idea of God and of salvation uprooted from their original Jewish source) which, besides turning them into Super-religions, on one hand forced them to create new foundations for their spiritual edifices, also in need of cultural moulds to give a body, a shape to their teachings; but on the other made them free from conditioning forms so that they were able to spread like fire presenting a message of total spiritual freedom. Hence their strong appeal to people who looked for a more rewarding inner response to their spiritual urges or who found in those a-cultural ways of life an escape from unpalatable (for them) socio-political frames. Thus, in India Buddhism was, at first, well received by kings who wanted to rule over a more homogeneous society or a more contented strata of population, but was finally reabsorbed into Brahmanism for those achievements that could be retained and definitely throw out of the country within a few centuries. It flourished in the farther East and South-East where it adapted itself to local costumes and cultures where these were most developed, like in China, or helped forging new ones when spreading in areas less culturally refined. The same happened with Christianity: thrown away from its Jewish couch almost at its start, found a most fertile soil in the provinces of the Roman Empire up to the Capital, satisfying with its spirituality two most prominent drives, besides others of course: an inner personal need for a deep spiritual urge when personal political involvement was no longer feasible, and a social support for a political opposition to the ruling Roman State. Islam followed in the same line, since the foreign feature of Mohammad's revelation left his followers without their tribal roots thus equally in need of new cultural settings and equally free to spread over other nations as a spiritual message. Such necessity of spreading outside their parent-land, coupled with the lack of 'national' roots, equipped these salvific messages with a missionary spirit seeking conversions right and left, thus ending up by dividing amongst themselves practically the whole world, where they reign almost undisturbed in their respective areas: East for Buddhism, South for Islam and North and West for Christianity. Only the tribal of the first group and the universalised national five or six of the third could stand their ground.

A further common cultural thread binding together these 'uprooted' messages of freedom and spiritual concern, is the great emphasis bestowed on their respective Founders. Lacking a cultural background feeding and absorbing any possible change fostered by other leaders, teachers and interpreters (as it is the case with China's great reformers, or Indian sadhus and gurus), the words of such Founders were the only and ultimate standpoints. It became, therefore, impossible to twist them or interpret them this way and that according to local and historical convenience. They had to be kept as faithfully as possible, so that almost from their start Councils were repeatedly held to keep check on their 'right' meaning, giving rise to Heresies when opinions varied and a majority was able to decide about the correct issue. Though, with the exception of Mohammad, neither of the other two Founders wrote a word, hip of sacred literature with their huge commentaries were put down recording every possible event, feature, sayings of the respective Lords. And that gave rise, first to a rigidity in keeping them authoritative and then to the need of strengthening them through Faith, which now changed its meaning from Trust to Belief. A further, common, consequence of their drastic cutting from a cultural milieu was the loss of a 'natural' nation able to give its people a feeling of 'belonging together' and, since this is a must in human relationship, the natural background has been substituted by the artificial regrouping into larger, supra-national, Communities (like the Sangham for the Buddhists, the Church (from the Greek work Ecclesia) for the Christians and the Ummah for the Muslims).

Anyway, with passing of time, those Communities supposed to be 'monolithic' blocks faithfully carrying on their Saviours' stands, could not avoid loosing control over different ways of interpreting and living the original messages of their Founders and each of them became a cluster of Sects, fighting each other in their claim to be the closer and more faithful preservers of their Founder's 'original' meaning.

5. In this last group are assembled those religions that sprung up as attempts to bridge the devastating effects of the spreading of the above mentioned spiritual Super-religions with the superseded local traditions, or with those traditions which did not allow themselves to be totally 'converted' or completely absorbed by them. The names of Sikhism, Bah'ai'ism, African syncretistic movements come readily to the mind. Most of them stem out either from Christianity or Islam, though also Buddhism must be pushing along its own syncretistic attempts.

Within this rather limited frame I think that all religions of the past and the present can find their own position, this helping the researchers and the seekers to draw the lines for comparison, valuation and discovery of certain particular inner developments as direct consequence of those religions' response to the historical drives that have determined their character so as to be included in one group instead of another. This also can explain certain 'strange' incongruities shared by some religions (especially the over-spread Super-religions) but not by others. Faith as Belief, an ideal fixity in a given Community, a group of Sacred Scriptures bearing strong weight in setting truths to be followed are some features which can be taken as examples. They match with the 'artificial' (because no longer arranged into 'natural' national roots) settings of the three great Spiritualities of the fourth group, but are not needed by the followers of the religious paths belonging to the previous three groups. In many comparative religion's books such bewildered discrepancies have been often put forward in prefaces in order to warn mainly Christian-influenced readers that what they consider a 'normal' feature is often not even present in whatever other tradition is going to be presented. In the perspective proposed herewith the position becomes inverted and the 'normal' way is rather that hold by those religions soundly rooted among their national people, so that it has no meaning to look for them in members of the other groups.

What is relevant for us here is that Brahmanism, with its exoteric opening into what is called today Hinduism, belongs to the second and then the third group, thus, historically sharing the needs of the other 'inmates' for forging a culture for their own people (belonging to a single nation, though never politically united under a single kingdom, not even today because beyond India political boundaries lay other states like Nepal, Pakistan, Indonesia, Bangladesh...belonging to its cultural range), for keeping certain unifying trends so that they can always recognise themselves as belonging to a given culture, and for being responsible of the guiding lines characterising them for themselves and in relation to the 'others', the 'aliens'.

Having then provided a broader chessboard to find the coordinates of Indian Heritage with respect to other cultural and spiritual Units, we shall proceed to tackle directly our subject matter.

ACKNOWLEDGEMENTS

I need to express my sincere thanks to all the people who have made possible the parturition and birth of this work. First, in order of chronology, my sister, Maria Emanuela, who, by reading the notes taken for a lecture delivered the task of reading in Rome in the early '90s and further elaborated in 1996/7 in this English translation, has suggested their publication and pushed strongly for it. Then, my great friend, professor Emeritus of B.H.U., Prof. J.N.Tiwari, who not only gave me valuable suggestions all along, but also shouldered upon himself the task of reading the typed scripts and furnished most of the references quoted in the footnotes. Thanks also to Mr Christopher N Burchett for carefully editing the whole lot and improving on the English language. Last but not least, thanks are due also to Miss Charu Chopra for painfully typing it out.

INTRODUCTION

1. Difference in terms.

Purposely I have introduced in the title a split between religion and spirituality in order to stress the distinct levels characterizing the relationship of man with that Power from which human life feels itself, willy nilly, dependent and conditioned upon. I take the first term somehow as the equivalent of the Sanskrit Dharma(taken from the Sanskrit root *dhr* meaning to support or uphold and developed from the earlier term *rita*, order, especially the cosmic and the divine), that is, I intend by it a system to put order in and to give a well-defined goal to the relationship of man with that superior Force which he feels surrounded by and dependent upon, on one side; and with his own fellow-beings—especially those of his own political and social group—on the other. I relate, instead, the other term, Spirituality (the Sanskrit term: *adhyâtma* can be taken as a good equivalent. It means: "inner core" or "inner sprit" as used in the Upanishads), to the personal situation of any individual, who struggles for the growth and realisation of his own personality adapting it, first, to a sound association with the others and, at the same time, harmonizing it from the inside with the exigencies of that mentioned Force. This one, in fact, though often remaining officially unnoticed and invisible, actually imparts an appreciable pressure on the individuals personality, a pressure that can hardly be ignored by any single perspective. This duality of levels is felt, more or less, in all human cultures, but in India it is more intensely perceivable because of the violence of its evidence, which is the violence specific to the Tropics' aggressiveness.

The two stages, however, do not oppose one another; rather they complement each other as two different steps in the growth of any community as well as of any individual. Each has its own value in the path of development and has to be attained at the right moment, without dangerous lingering in the strict religious social order when individuals have reached inner maturity and autonomy or without pressing for a premature freedom from the rules governing their lives when individuals have yet to be fully developed. Both are, therefore, necessary and have to be respected in the differentiation of their relative paths. In India such paths cross each other in society and human life with more frequency and stronger evidence than in other countries and civilizations, because of its geographical tendency to stress the extremes and because of the strong relevance given *tour-à-tour* to the role of society and to the realized individuals inside it.

2. Culture as a way to control Reality

Since, as we are going to see, India's geographical setting can be defined as a "superabundant multiplicity over a background of Void", the main task facing such a culture which feels itself called to cope with that kind of situation without however loosing a claim to an inner unity, is that to harness such a multiplicity into a net similar to that of meridians and parallels cast over a geographical map, so as to give to such a Nature a kind of reference point to be taken as a guide to the complexity of its cultural and social intricacies. At the same time, this very net would be a sort of 'guiding-line' slowly leading individuals to build themselves up in such a way as to be fit to face the underlying Void without succumbing to the terror normally produced by its engulfing abyss. All this, from the point of view of a practical realization of life, can be synthesized by the bi-polarity expressed in the title: i.e. the necessity of a cultural/religious (social and collective) order properly grounded on well organized and rigid foundations, placed as it were before the other equally necessary extreme: the absolute freedom of the individual personality, when somebody has reached the inner maturity needed for it.

3. Scheme of the work

In this respect, India may rightly claim to have reached, during centuries and even millennia of application, a balanced blend of the two modes of inner life, which we are going to examine; and, since the geographical position played a determinant role in shaping the culture and the religious reactions of its inhabitants, we are going to start our task by having a look at its geographical and climatic coordinates, following which, not unlike a Mandala grounded on a basic fourfold division according to a traditional enumeration of 3+1, we shall present, as the second feature, the Normative

Coordinates in their social order (*castes*), temporal division (*yugas*), individual concerns and stages (*ashramas*) together with their respective aims, (artha), their 'sacramental' rites *(sanskaras)* coupled with the theory of debts, (*rina*), with the conception of Death and with the related Law of Karma, as the 7th; the Religious Coordinates in their sacrificial order rooted in the Vedas and responsible for Vedic norms and spread at a popular level into the Myths of Pauranic knowledge, would be our third point. This scheme is, then, completed with a fourth and inherently different element: the Spiritual Dimension, concerning especially the individual walk on personal paths, practically concretised in the canonical three spiritual Margas: Karma, Jnana and Bhakti. A conclusion will sum up this necessarily very short panorama, which is meant more as a catching of the spirit behind this complete religious and spiritual structure, rather than as an attempt at an exhaustive presentation. This 'exhaustiveness' would be practically impossible to attain because of the immensity of the subject to be covered and of the numberless little streams and rivers and rivulets in which the spiritual waters of Brahmanism and Hinduism had divided and spread themselves out practically since the very beginning of their 'history' or, better, development.

Though we have tried to include as many items as it was humanly possible, nevertheless many could only hardly be touched upon, others merely mentioned, while still others (like Tantrism, for instance) had to be ignored because of their inner complexity and wholesomeness, requiring a specialised study. Also philosophical schools have been left out because their relation with religious matters is more on an intellectual and speculative standard, even if it cannot be said that they disregard practical behaviour and personal involvement.

PART I

PART I

CHAPTER 1
Geographical Setting.

Geographically, India is a country of vastness, where everything stands limitless without boundaries and the horizons stretch monotonously on all sides, uninterrupted, whatever their content: plains, mountains, a river's meanders, rocks or jungle. These immense distances, even enhanced by a sky generally clear and, in its diffuse and rarefied glow, rather further away than in more compact landscapes (as in Southern Europe for instance), are more apt to let their inhabitants perceive the Void which appears to be in the background of such extended display of vastness. And Void is very hard to behold for the common psychology of average man; without an adequate preparation, facing it normally produces to individual and societies a feeling of vertigo, of dizziness, of being lost altogether.

India is, moreover, placed in the Tropics, which means that it is also subjected to a ferocious impulse of growth leading globally to an overflowing abundance in all fields. That is to say that these immense distances are filled up to the brim with every form of life: of vegetation, insects, beasts and human beings, so that a cultured man, since almost at the beginning of the emergence of his consciousness, finds himself overwhelmed by such plenty. In this sense, India can be considered the country where the 'Too Much' stands as if suspended on Void; a condition very difficult to be faced by average people, because the 'Too Much' risks engulfing individuals and groups alike, while Void tends to suck up the single persons evoking in them, when not properly fortified, the fear of psychological dissolution.[1]

NOTES

1. The same considerations can be found in A. L. Basham, *The Wonder that was India*, London, 1954 p.3-4 though he declares himself not agreeing with this view.

CHAPTER 2
Climatically

Climatically also India is faced with the same problem of 'Too Much'. The fact of being at the Tropics subjects its territories to cyclical climatic excesses with a minimum of bearable transitory periods. Nothing like the comfortable moderation of the countries placed in what are called 'temperate zones'. In India when it is winter the cold, at least in the North, reaches almost the freezing point with loss of lives in people usually not adequately protected; during summer, the thermometer shoots up to 45°, 50° (of meteorological bulletins, which means at least 55° in the shadow in villages and in the congested city-areas) with a further toll of lives. But when, at last, the most invoked rain starts its proper season, very often it does not only rain, but it pours down without measure so that more likely than not floods will follow, with consequently further loss of human and animal lives. If, however, rain did not overflow there is the not less feared risk of drought with long time consequences of lack of cultivation and of food for the year to come.

In this way also climate, with its excesses but also with its regularly re-proposal of the same conditions over and over again, contributes to put Indians before a chronically feeling of insecurity, making them perceive the 'Too Much' in its recurring crisis with a despairing sense of 'an eternal return', fixing up into immobility, almost as in a sclerosis, its whirling coming back of ineluctable seasonal cycles; this leading to the conception of an endless, eternal time indefinitely repeating itself for ever.

CHAPTER 3
Sum up

To sum it up, one can say that India, with its over-crowded territories hanging over a Void yawning behind its distances and coupled, at the same time, with the devastating climatic crisis periodically chasing one another with a hopeless regularity, put a leading group of people to face the necessity of finding a meaning to an immutable yet impermanent reality over the background of a repetitious stability of weather, which allowed a glimpse into the eternal. In other words, India pushed the propounders of its main culture to find a suitable interpretation capable of neutralizing the potentially psychological damage of a "nature full of 'Too Much' suspended over an abyss of Void" as a *sine qua non* for surviving such a situation, which could be devastating for the psychical balance of average people, whose mentality could be obviously at ease only within a finite time and in a space measurable according to manageable parameters.

One has to add that these conditions were more easily met within tribal circles where only the territory surrounding their villages really mattered, while the vastness beyond it was safely exorcised through a wise isolation within a more controllable inhabited area. At the same time, by cutting off the immensity of the horizons, also the presence of the Void with its inherent potentiality of Sacredness became less terrifying and more easily convertible into more or less personified Forces liable to be invoked for help or appeased with rites. With the same stroke, the dangerousness of seasonal changes is kept relatively tamed by the limitedness of a selected home, which does not leave room for comparison and thus circumscribes, as it were, the chances of destructivity. The perception of such vastness in its terrific dimensions beyond measure, coupled with an unmanageable diversity in all realms of life and nature, would instead be felt with utmost intensity by those people who, following the need of always new pastures for their cattle and horses began to step over the large and undifferentiated territories of Indian plains. This could put a tread to the people religiously in charge of their tradition, who did not dream accepting to loose their inner cohesion and their cultural solidarity. Only people of this kind could have had the possibility of becoming aware of the immensity of the land they were crossing, together with the whirling diversity of all forms of life imbued in it and the deadly fury of Tropical seasons, which, though never uniformly dangerous, were nevertheless always striking with violence either one part or the other of the whole country. The people so challenged were the bearers of the 'Vedic culture' and undoubtedly they were able to meet their challenge.

Before proceeding farther, however, it is advisable to add a warning and point out another limitation of this essay. The situation we are presenting here, with climatic excesses vastness of space, diversity in populations and in flora and fauna, is essentially based on conditions prevailing in Northern India; so also cultural and religious dealings with them mostly refer to what went on and still goes on in that part of this huge country. South India is rather different in many respects, therefore also cultural and religious reactions to the surroundings tend, obviously, to be of another kind with respect to the dominant current developed in the North. Most of these differences are, often, attributed to a different layer of population, coming from local folk: the Dravidians. This is surely correct and Dravidians are distinguishable from the Northern 'Aryan' folks in feature, colour and languages together with their scripts; nevertheless, it is also undeniable that they were amply Sanskritised and Brahmanised very early in history, so much so that in many respects it is in the South— especially Andhra Pradesh and Tamil Nadu, Karnataka, Maharashtra and Banaras in the state of Uttar Pradesh—that the most orthodox tradition is to be found and in a better preserved manner. Yet, the land, the people in it, more uniform weather condition and less vastness to be lost in, have all contributed to give even to the Brahmanic South a different aspect all together. There, festivals are celebrated in a different manner, often even changing the actual dates (for instance, Dipawali that is commemorated on the following Full Moon instead of the New Moon day as celebrated in the North) or in the difference of their names, therefore, in the purpose implied in them (as Pongal which is kept at the place of Makara Sankranti the 13th of January), and the like. Since, in any case, Vedic culture is without much controversy considered to come from the mountains of North-West India[1], to spread steadily and fast over the Gangetic plains and the Deccan plateau, and only in a second movement reached the South, we prefer to maintain the standard fashion of dealing with Sanskrit culture and Vedic cum Hindu religions as followed in Northern India.

NOTES

1   The origins of Indian people have been a controversial issue since the beginning of Western interest in the subject. For an exhaustive survey of the matter—to which we shall come later—see E. Bryant, *The Quest for the Origins of Vedic Culture. The Indo-Aryan Migration Debate*. Oxford (O.U.P) 2001

PART II
COORDINATES AS NORMATIVE RULES

CHAPTER 1
The people responsible for such coordinates

Actually, nobody properly knows wherefrom these people exactly came. The most common theory is that their homeland could have been somewhere in the Caucasus mountains; it was, at any rate, a place—judging by the nouns and names left in inheritance to Indo-European folks—covered with oak forests and mighty rivers, hence they moved in recurrent waves toward the South-East and the West and North-West roughly around the years 2000-1500 BC. Their average characteristics were: fairness of complexion[1], mastery over horses with the related chariot-driving techniques, and especially a common basic language divided, probably since the beginning of their history, in several connected dialects. Together with it they also shared a roughly common Pantheon and a rather uniform culture, with Fire having the main role in the performance of their rituals as well as for its use as a weapon. Most likely, however, this racially and somehow culturally compact people never belonged to a unified nation; they seem rather to have consisted of many groups, often fighting one another, and moving at random in their nomadic quest for new pasture for their cattle—their main source of wealth—and for juicy booty to be looted. Their first sweeping over Europe and some parts of the Middle East is documented around the above mentioned dates, which may be safely be assumed to be also that of their spreading over Iran and India—or at least to their coming into power here[2]. This has to be specified because there is now, in India, a strong tendency among local scholars to claim autochthony for the bearers of Vedic culture, quasi as having them crossing the borders from outside sometime about over four millennia ago would continue to keep them as·'foreigners' to their own land, notwithstanding the fact that they became what they are only after having reached Indian soil and after having had to properly cope with it. As this seems to be such a vital issue, I feel that there would be no harm to enlarge the supposed original Caucasian region into including the mountains of

Afghan and North Pakistan, giving thus to the horse-tamers the right of legitimately belonging where they rightly became the moulders of Vedic and Sanskrit culture[3]—since it is, as it has been said, only in India that these connected groups of people developed the culture and the way of life known as Brahmanism and even later as Hinduism. In any case, one thing can be rather safely attested: though essentially not alien to the Indian North-Western milieu, the 'Aryan' tribes who reached political and cultural supremacy over the whole subcontinent were only one part of the entire population whom they endeavour to unify into a harmonious cultural and religious whole, while respecting at the same time the diversities proper to the Tropical 'Too Much'. And this situation, by the way, would remain valid even if the theory of an unlikely derivation from the Harappa and Mohanjo Daro's civilization could be eventually proved.[4]

Be it as it may, these groups of people, though never forming a single political unit, while moving South and Eastward in their restless nomadic wandering after their cattle gradually came in contact with the vastness of the plains, filled with people intrinsically different from themselves, and marked by the overflowing abundance of the Tropics just described. They had, therefore, to come into terms with situations different from those they were accustomed to, that is to say they had to learn how to deal with the plenty of a very fertile soil coupled with differentiation in climatic conditions and with the amazing fecundity of all sort of animals, insects and human beings (who, generally, we may suppose hostile to the belligerent new comers from the mountains) without, however, loosing their cultural unity. (The Rig Veda especially, but also the other Vedas, are clearly referring to many different groups, speaking the same language, but fighting each other, still their poets and priests are the one shifting from group to group and, though acknowledging alliances and enmity among them, strive to keep a cultural unity, as shall be seen later on.)

This was, in fact, the main force behind building the entire Sanskrit cultural edifice: namely, the desire to preserve a strong link among themselves through the maintenance of a single culture, and possibly a single learned language, common to all. Keeping such bound entailed, first of all, the realization of the existence of a large scale disparity now striking them right in the face not only with respect to alien aborigines but, through contact with them, also with respect to the differences suddenly showing themselves up within their own groups. These had to be maintained at least to a certain degree in order to suit the needed articulation of a society ready to settle down into a sedentary style of life (entailing a diversification of expertise, therefore of people acquiring the skill, culture and world-view proper to their different particular specializations), but at the same time had to be blended into an over-embracing unity covering as it were all political, national and social diversifications characterizing their racial folks. Furthermore, besides bridging somehow the multifarious shapes of the 'Too Much' appearing now to them with all its difficulties, the rising dominant 'race' had also to find a way to prepare, as we have seen, its individuals to endure the psychologically unbearable glimpses of the Void transpiring in between and behind the dilatation of Space and Time, or else to resist its untiming attraction. And all this had to be attended to in such a way as to be made quite sure that the same kind of cultural interpretation would be shared by all their groups, though at different levels and various degrees of understanding according to the respected rule of the diversity fostered by the above mentioned 'Too Much'. And one has to acknowledge that they were up to the task, which they tackled in the manner suitable for all the people belonging to that age and to the religious group presented as N.2: through religious rites.

Rites, in fact, were the operative modes of humanity, till the era of science and technicality took over in the so-called 'modern world'. They were performed not so much for the sake of "pleasing" or even "feeding" the various Deities—as many an external observer may often understand these practices—but rather as a mean for involving the Divine into providing or even 'creating' a proper order out of the amorphous 'chaos'[5] of the Wilderness. In India, as seen, such chaos, though the most commonly used term comes from another culture[6] was so powerful as to be most of the time self-evident. But equally powerful were the Vedic rituals too, especially in their form called Yajna. Here around the culminating act of pouring the offering into the Fire a complete structure of the world was devised and fixed up, reminding as it were the manner of throwing a net of coordinates, parallels and meridians like, over life and society in order to get points of reference at any moment and occurrence.

The result of this enormous effort has been kept in the conceptions devised in ancient times and transmitted by the Sacred Word of the Vedas together with a well developed doctrine of the connected sacrificial Action (*yajna*) which, through the ages, has slowly risen to become that multifarious religion called Hinduism or, in the local term: *sanatana dharma*, the "Eternal Law", the main subject-matter of our presentation.[7]

NOTES
1. This can be (inferred) surmised by the fact that stills nowadays the parameter for beauty and handsomeness is "fairness".

2. See M Vannucci, *Human Ecology in the Vedas* N. Delhi (D K Printworld) 1999, pp 31

3. The Indian Sanskrit is the language of the learned pandits and sages (Rishis); there is also a more popular form (prakrita) and the similarities both in terms, grammars and syntactical structures, with other European and Iranian peoples (also having myths that point towards an Immigration from the East or the North-East) make them pertaining to the same broader family of people. This similarity has been studied for the last two centuries, beginning with the well known figure of F. Max-Muller.

4. See the already quoted controversy in E Bryant *op cit*

5. Chaos in fact is a Greek term; a Sanskrit equivalent in difficult to trace. Perhaps the term Pralaya is the closet to be found, but it means rather "dissolution", "disorder" as opposed to creation.

6. I refer here to a debate started on political bases and finally summarized by the quoted book of E Bryant.

7. See later on. This essay, actually, is founded on Yajna (Sacrifice) and its effects as on all levels: cultural, religious and spiritual (through its break through).

CHAPTER 2
Social Structure: caste system.

The description of the above mentioned sacrificial action, Yajna, shall be dealt with at its proper place in the chapter dealing with religion as such; here, however, some of its bearings over the social construction have to be proposed, since also this presentation has to maintain a kind of internal order in which the political and social structure should be kept to the front so as to form the background or the foundations of the whole. It has to be said, to begin with, that usually the performance of a Yajna in its solemn form was, already in ancient times when it was a matter of serious concern and of vital importance, seldom celebrated and only on very special occasions. Nevertheless, when it did occur under the patronage (today one could perhaps say under the sponsorship) of some victorious and influential prince or king (raja) or of some very rich traders or some brahmans very highly placed in the ministry of some kingdom, it was such an event that engaged for years the whole officiating class not only in the preparation and execution of the rites to be actually performed, but especially in the arduous and trying task of understanding, explaining and interpreting the full Action, both in its entirety and in each of its items. This was vital because nothing could be left to chance due to the world-wide influence of the Sacred Action with repercussions in the whole Universe. Any mistake could lead to disaster reverberating, if not properly and timely checked, in waves throughout the cosmos, and, at the same time, any careless movement or any false step in the proceedings, if not fully circumscribed and properly redressed, could contribute to build up a wrong cultural world in which to live.

Though in principle any Yajna was performed on behalf of an individual sponsor with his wife, who were the pre-eminent beneficiary of the material benefits to be obtained (usually a son, victory in battle, increase in wealth, and eventually an immortal body with which to be able to enter paradise, (svarga), there was also a broader meaning attached to it: it was supposed to literally "weave" the texture of the World. It settled the *Rita*, the supernatural as well as the legal "Order" forming the parameters of a righteous life and behaviour. The Sanskrit term *rita* is connected with its Latin counterpart *ordo*, also meaning "order", but which is also related to the term *orditus* the "warp" in a tissue. Thus, the *Rita* produced by Yajna is also the Principle governing the performance of the Sacred Action, and extends its field of power into casting the coordinates of righteous and moral behaviour for human society on one side, and of the cosmic laws for an ordained and balanced proceeding in Universe, on the other[1].

With respect to human society, this "woven" reality serves the purpose of taming or regulating the chaotic realm of multiplicity into a workable and liveable world. It somehow 'compartmentalizes' it into manageable units, suited to cope with the variety of the 'Too Much', yet maintaining a kind of underlying oneness befitting the 'Aryan' strong sentiment of "belonging together". This was translated into practice on a horizontal as well as vertical dimension. Horizontally: in so far as the holders of the Vedic culture never formed a political unity, but were divided in small kingdoms ruled by royal families assisted by a large hierarchy of ministers and advisers, thus forming a cluster of politically differentiated areas with a 'national' feeling of sharing the same cultural world. India became a unified political nation only after gaining back her freedom from the British hardly sixty years ago; even the conquerors during their rule in the country respected her structure in small kingdoms. And this is so strongly inherent to this culture that even today the Indian nation does not cover the whole area of Brahmanic cultural influence, which, as said before, spread outside her boundaries into Nepal, Pakistan, Bangladesh, Burma, part of Indonesia (in the Island of Bali especially) in somehow a direct way, and even farter East and South East Asia through Buddhist influence. In this way such political arrangement reduced somehow the spell produced by the immensity of geographical distances. But sedentary life after a certain period is apt to produce differences even inside the bulk of population, either through a branching out of various specialized duties and occupations, or through close interlocking relations with local populations slowly absorbed into the new pattern of life, or through both. Such differences too had, therefore, to be dealt with and kept under control, especially in their mushrooming steady expansion. This took the form of a vertical division in what later on became settled as the "caste system", which is mainly grounded on specialization of work (reminding us of European medieval trade guilds) and on large family's and groups' relations linked together by a common trading tradition entailing distinctive social and ritual behaviours.

Though rather looked down upon by modern Westernised people and by the socialistic equalizing trend, and in spite of being undoubtedly open to undue abuses and exploitation, this internal division of society has nevertheless played an important role in getting India through a good many invasions, cultural and religious influences, disrupting forces trying to tear apart her cohesion...in a word, it gave its culture the possibility of keeping its features intact without loosing the treasure of her cultural wealth. Castes also preserved India's cultural wealth of plurality by regulating its flow through a variety of canals, meant for the survival of specifically local cultures and traditions; while, at the same time, through the interlock of such canals, they could recognise their basic unity, since it was the same water which ran in them. Moreover, in the frightening overflowing of Tropical excesses, the caste system avoided a shapeless haphazard confusion where any single unit could get irretrievably lost— and so becoming either a non-entity whom nobody would care for, or a maniac after power in order to emerge from oblivion. Seen in this perspective, caste division has been a way to reach a difficult balance between preserving a kind of underlying unity, and, at the same time, a valid means to save the identity of every single group in which any individual can recognise his position and feel a sense of solidarity with his equals.[2]

Anyway, there should have been, as it were, a positive value attached to this social division because, in spite of so much grouching and despising, coupled with its formal abolition by the Constitution of Indian Nation, the caste system still maintains its strong grip on the social structure. It is true, however, that, especially in the last ten-twenty years, it's more orthodox rules about purity and impurity have been rather relaxed while life in big cities provided a way to escape its more rigid application as followed in villages, thus rendering its negative points less troublesome[3]. Notwithstanding its many drawbacks, the caste system perhaps resists because caste solidarity protects individuals in their daily needs, especially when hardship hits them, and above all safeguards an individual's personality by surrounding it with the presence of others of the same group. Thereby, it gives each of them the sense of belonging to something concrete, without the feeling of being lost in the psychological unbearable sense of general indifference as generated by the 'Too Much'. Even physically Indians often give the impression of fearing and hating solitude so that one generally finds them in bunches, often seating themselves so closely to one another as almost to defeat the physic law of impenetrability of bodies—except for the not uncommon exceptions of religious ascetics who seek solitude for spiritual reasons, and possibly just in the way of contrast or compensation.

The groups (*jata*) raised by such internal division of Indian society, reach several thousands but are roughly distributed into four main groups[4], following a traditional pattern of enumeration in 3+1 about which we shall discuss later.

They are the well known: —

Brahmins, with educational and priestly tasks of preservation and transmission of the basic tenets of their culture and of what concern sacred items;

Kshatriyas, trusted with the task of ruling and defending their states and nations;

Vaisyas, dealing with trade and commerce thus holding practically the bulk of riches of their countries.

The members of these three main castes enjoying the rights of full citizenship inside their kingdoms and with respect to the wider Indian territory; they are also called the "twice born" (*dvija*) because they are entitled to perform a kind of initiatory ceremony which is equivalent to a second birth with social and religious implications.

Apart from them, there is also a fourth caste (the +1 of the pattern) that of the *Sudra*s, giving shelter to all the other communities, scattered from the respected cattle raisers (Ahir and Yadava) and scribes (Srivastava, Mathur etc.) down to those bordering the lowest levels like the laundry-men (dhobi) and barbers (nau), passing through a very wide gamut of them. They form the class of artisans, small agriculturists, public and private servants engaged in various kinds of jobs and small sized trade. They form, obviously, the greatest part of the population and today they are rising fast on the political scale.

All those that, for one reason or another, do not find a place in this well-defined network, belong to the even vaster category of the "outcast". The greatest part of such "outcasts" is those who are racially different and cannot be blended into that organic whole: the tribal still living in many regions grouped in villages of their own and the 'foreigners' in general. Among the foreigners, however, the 'white people' enjoy a kind of privilege, because, though outcasts and impure like the average strangers, they still belong roughly to the same kinship that once migrated to the West more or less in the same period of their coming into power on Indian soil. The other groups of people labelled as 'outcast' belong perhaps to the same racial and cultural stock, but by performing jobs putting them in contact with very impure objects—like human excrement for instance, or the skins of dead animals—they cannot find place in any of the well compartmentalized social divisions. They work, indeed, in the mist of society but are restricted in their dealing with its higher members not having access to their houses except through the back door for reaching the latrines, not being allowed to touch their water and their fire, or to touch kitchen utensils and the like. Of course, in these days of social equality such restrictions seem unfair and absurd, but also here there is a touch of that overflowing multiplicity and abundance that is behind the utter impossibility to get a firm control over proper behaviour. Who, for instance, may be absolutely sure that a person, having just cleaned a dry latrine, has got the leisure and the means to properly wash his/her hands? Can such a person be allowed to pollute the water my children or I are going to drink? To be on the safer side—and this with more strength during ancient times in which there was not much protection against unhygienic behaviour— better to keep them at a distance. Also ritual Purity can become a serious problem on given religious occasions.

In India, of course, especially in the very ancient times, there could not be question of a sense of hygiene as understood now, but its culture had always kept a very keen sense of distinction between pure and impure items, and this is strong even today. For the greatest part we may fairly say that the two points of view often are identical; nevertheless the differences are also quite noticeable. The category of purity or of impurity is applied with various degrees to things, people, anatomical parts of the body, food, and the like, so that dealing with them all in different moments and situations entails a whole system of procedures and precautions. There are rules for eating, drinking, relieving nature; rules about the parts of the body that have to be used on certain occasions and for certain functions; rules for cooking, for dressing, for washing oneself and one's clothes and one's dishes; rules about dealing with people, about approaching the Deities or anything sacred; and rules extended to handle the different types of work and jobs held up in any society.

All these rules are often difficult and cumbersome and therefore cannot be imposed with the same rigidity and meticulousness to all the members of such an articulated society as the Indian one. The higher the members the most dependable they are considered to be; therefore they can be properly trusted for their sincerity and willingness to keep up with the law of purity by avoiding impurity as far as possible and by properly cleansing themselves when avoidance is out of the question. The lower the caste the lesser the trust in them, therefore the smaller the burden which would be placed on their shoulders; yet the penalty is that of being set aside from the main social stream of life[5]. But this is not a totally unusual feature in many a nation and people, including modern ones, where members of the same class of work, education and income stick together in social exchanges, and where absolute equality can never be reached as the difference is embedded in nature as well as in any articulated society.

Another feature of the caste system is its ability to preserve special customs proper to each group, for example, songs, festivals, myths, Deities, behavioural trends and traditions which have only caste solidarity as an adequate means of transmission from generation to generation, since common schooling and education cannot take into account all these endless rivers and rivulets of cultural diversity, which are in themselves a treasure of indescribable value. Also some of the hardship for which India is known to the world—for instance the fate of widows who cannot marry again and have a difficult and unwanted chastity to maintain—are mainly valid for the members of the three high castes but has no hold with those belonging to the fourth—who can not only re-marry their widows but also accept divorce and re-marriage for the female folk as well. The main drawback of this structure remains the tendency of despising the 'lower' stock. There are some considerations though to keep in mind: since the concept of purity and impurity is the main drive behind caste division, Brahmans are usually regarded as the highest of all but, due to their pre-eminent task of dealing with the sacrosanct and not with material matters, their resultant poverty does not always allow them to enjoy in practice that high respect that tradition wants us to believe that they are entitled to; on the other hand, also due to the equally distributed opportunities of getting rich through many kinds of new jobs and political careers, some members of the lower caste claim such a respect through sheer monetary and sometimes even physical strength and power. Again, therefore, we are in the presence of the worldwide experience that, in the end, what really counts is individual aptitude and personality, coupled with one's capacity of mastering a good financial wealth and property.

Moreover, this caste structure could be equated to a mansion of many rooms each assigned to the performance of certain work so that change from one another are made virtually almost impossible, nevertheless some limited shifts are sometimes allowed, especially when lower caste members migrate from villages to cities and get jobs in levelling factories, trade or offices, or, even better, enter government through the vehicle of trade-unions, or, on the other hand, when, due to the intermediary of "pure" machinery, people of high caste do not disdain opening businesses in dry-cleaning (normally left to laundrymen) or in chemical tanning factories (previously the exclusive work of outcasts). And this is valid not only socially, but, strangely enough since such a division has a strong religious foundation; it holds possibilities of a break even in its spiritual domain. As we are going to see later on, the caste system is not even an inexorable barrier for spiritually advanced people who can jump to freedom from whatever position they chance to occupy in their last dwelling in this phenomenal world.

NOTES

1. For all the details and the proper description of Yajna see further at its proper place. References on caste are to be found even in the late Rigveda; see e.g. RV I, 164, ff: X. 90, 12; X.130.1-2; etc.

2. Before entering into a detailed description of this inner cultural and social division it is advisable to remind the reader that, though the caste system seem to devise a descending gradation of Values, these are based mostly (if not exclusively) on "purity" concept and not on degree of power or even respectability. Often it is noted that the members of whatever caste are very proud of their status—even if officially ranked in lower positions.

3. And this was valid also in ancient terms where pandits (the holders of caste purity) warned against the relaxation of the cities dwellers, as it is clear from the Dharma Sástra literature

4. On caste there is a vast literature, out of which we can quote: P.V. Kane *History of Dharma Shastra*, Vol. II, Chts I- IV. J.H. Hutton, *Caste in India*, (OUP) Bombay 1963; P. H. Prabhu, *Hindu Social Organization-A Study in Socio-psychological and Ideological Foundation*, Bombay 1963; M. N. Srinivas, *Caste in Modern India and other Essays*, Bombay 1964 (4th ed.) R. Lannoy, *the Speaking Tree, A Study of Indian Culture and Society*, Oxford (OUP) 1970 (2nd 1976) part III. And the classic L. Dumont, *Homo Hierarchicus: The Caste System and its Implications*, rev. ed. and Translation. Chicago (Ch. U.P) 1980.

5. Though it is worthwhile to reinstate that if "despise" is involved from the "high" class toward the "low", it can be detected the other way also. I can never forget the look of total disapproval of a tribal (Santhal) toward the upper class people (and professors) playing joyfully in colour splashing Holi Festival (See later), and the sense of superiority of a tribal man from Ranchi towards the despised Hindu. See also the satirical novel (not appreciated by Brahmans) by U. R. Anantha Murthy, *Sanskaras: A rite for a dead man*, Delhi (OUP) 1978.

CHAPTER 3
Temporal Structure

a. Cycle of seasons

If vastness of space and the multi-faced variety of the Indian populace have pushed the culturally dominant groups to find a way of harnessing multiplicity in a manner that could allow diversity to be interwoven into a basic form of unity; so also the frightening sequence of violent Tropical seasons, with their endless repetition of destructive extremes, had to be somehow explained and interpreted so as to be made more bearable for the survivors. Their violence, as we have seen in the previous chapter, has the psychological effect of breeding a feel of incertitude in life—one can never be sure of being able to get through a wave of unbearable heat or of excessive cold or to survive floods or to have the resources to endure a famine brought about by drought—but the eventual end of the trouble fostering the never failing coming back of intermediary mild situations before falling again into the contrary excesses, also lead to an hopeful and at the same time despairing sense of an inexorable endless repetitiousness apt to drive people mad.

i) Festivals

Thus, the people responsible for cultural unity endeavoured to bridle and tame seasons in the same way as they had coped with overflowing social variety: through rituals. Yajna, by weaving cosmic order into reality, built up an organized cultural system and within that system also many a turbulent weather display could be brought to reason by engaging the responsibility of cosmic forces involved in it (like the Maruts and the Rudras, for example)(See RV I. 85.5 for the Maruts). But Yajna was never a regularly performed sacred action and in any case only a small given portion of the leading people could be brought to interfere with Nature through this means. Other layers of population were naturally willing to be put in the position to handle those seasons whose havoc was of more concern for them than for the upper and wealthy class. Furthermore, with the passage of time and change in political and social setting, Yajna performances became even rarer, so that, even for such 'privileged' ones, rites had to be supplied to join in and get benefits from. Such rites were seasonal festivals, which have counterparts all over the world in every religion worth its name. These are popular ceremonies involving everybody in his (or her) own capacity and have the same power of weaving order in seasonal succession, by measuring their constant coming back through stressing certain temporal key-points, generally positioned around Equinoxes and Solstices[1]. These points became in their turn the key-knots holding the years into shape like in a carpet's texture. And since in India everything has the tendency of being considered as a whole and all levels are somehow interconnected, so many important festivals are driven towards becoming the beginning of the year starting after their happening in a manner that put them in the position of New Year Days, with the end result that their plurality has to be distributed evenly among the castes. Each of the four-caste group, therefore, can count on a yearly beginning of its own on which to adjust their further rites, while the whole lot gets its share of them on different grounds and premises. An example of this situation can be the festival of Raksha Bandana taken by all Hindus as celebrating a temporary reunion between brothers and sisters (with the latter bound for once to go back to their parental home, which especially in ancient time and still among traditional villagers was and is a coveted and welcome opportunity) but for Brahmins alone it acquires the status of the beginning of a new year in which they renovate their vows and put on anew the mark of their Brahmanhood together with new garments; the festival falls during the rainy season. Another example can be the novena starting with the new moon of the month of Ashvina (roughly falling between middle of September and middle October thus meeting somehow the requirements of Fall Equinox) and culminating with the Tenth Day (Dassehra) where the Deity—either in the form of Rama if people are celebrating it according to the saga of Vishnu or in the form of Durga, if the celebrants follow the saga of the Goddess connected with Shiva's world—conquers Evil so as to free mankind from it, at least for another year; because of its link with fight this festival is naturally connected with the Kshetriya groups who celebrate with it their own New Year start. As for the Vasya their starting point will come at the next immediate New Moon Day celebrated in all Northern India as Dipavali, or the Festival of Lights, but which they charge with their own meaning renewing on that day their account books and their business activities. The beginnings for the Sudras is assumed by the festivities of Holi, celebrating with colourful disorder the Spring Equinox ending the hard wintertime and introducing the fast coming summer. Meanwhile, Spring was already welcomed some forty days before Holi with the season festival of Vasant Panchami (the fifth Day of February Moon) attached, in Hindu mythology, to the Goddess of Learning, Sarasvati, and therefore especially dear to students, teachers and scholars. And winter, in its somewhat delayed Solstice (here falling on the 13th January) is celebrated with the eating of a special dish and a feverish play of kites.

When the Hindu Pantheon got firmly established (as we are going to see later on), then all the main Deities were entitled to have their own festivities celebrated either during the days of the week or the month with a special emphasis once a year: so for Shiva, Rama, Krishna, Hanuman, Ganesh, Lakshmi, Kali...[2]. In between all this heavily scheduled festive calender, some space remains for private functions, like marriage and coming of age ceremonies—the only sacramental (samskara) happenings that can be held at properly chosen moments, since births and deaths do not bother to keep convenient times! Anyway, festivals, though officially common to all and meant to foster human sociality, are *de facto* dealt with mostly in the individuality of private family nucleuses.

The diversification of time based on changes in weather bears also on the opening up of pilgrimages, another important feature of every culture of the world and of India in particular, which shall be briefly dealt with later in the chapter about Religion as such. Pilgrimages try somehow to concentrate space and time in some special spots, which for one reason or another are conceived as more suitable for being open canals between this world of everyday life and that representing the vast Infinity of the Divine. Myths are often connected with them generally explaining the choice of the spot together with the particular time selected for a better and more complete advantage in venturing forth on such type of trips.

ii) Yugas

Now, festivals, with their regular occurrence year after year propose again and again the same topics. They also bring about the same renewals, the same getting rid of the old, of heaviness, of exhausted, worn out energies so as to be able to replenish them again in plenty putting them in a position to start all over again the process of endless depletion and get them ready for new refuelling. This lead the sages, responsible for cultural and religious setting, to face the threat of Void, which eternity (or endlessness in seasonal cycles) re-proposes on a time basis in more or less the same proportion in which vastness of space lets it surface through the monotony of distant horizons.

Time, in fact, if taken as a straight line (as among the Hebrews, for instance, that have a starting point in the creation of their God and a final goal to be reached at the end of their worldly journeys), is naturally bound to come sooner or later to one form or other of an end, of a completeness. But, also if taken as a circular movement according to seasons and astronomical revolutions of the sun through the zodiacal signs (as among the Greeks, the Romans and the Chinese, just to take a few examples) it can make allowances for methods of linear counting by differentiating various periods either through the marks of accumulating Olympic Games (among the Greeks) or through the names of political people in power during its various moments, as the Romans did, or by enumerating the various kings in their succeeding dynasties, as it happened among the ancient Egyptians, Chinese and others. This circularity, then, appears to be completed in it and at the same time it could be stretched, so to say, into an historical—or rather historio-graphical—linearity, which could endeavour to have events properly distinguished, and as such dated. This precise counting, at its turn, prevents time to open up toward a frightful eternal dimension.

This dimension, instead, is fully present in Indian climatic conditions and spacious surroundings. Uncertainty of life constantly threatening individuals and kingdoms compelled them both to concentrate all their efforts to survive the present, while the repetitious coming back of the same catastrophic seasons marked by the endless return of the same festivals, compelled the builders of Indian culture to become aware of the boredom behind this perpetual roundabout, which, however, on a short-term standard can never be taken totally for granted so as to allow within a human life-time a proper planned future to be looked forward at with expectation. Again, therefore, in the same manner that has been worked out for making space and multiplicity endurable, also time had to be made at least countable in order for it to be brought down to human measure, but in such a way as to maintain visible the spellbound immensity of its unimaginable length, suggested by its seasonal rhythms. The result of all this took the form of a division in yugas equivalent more or less with the cosmic ages of Hesiod only assuming a breathtaking proportion.

These Yugas with their staggering enumeration were less prominent as such in the Vedic and even Brahmanic times. The names later used for designing them and the ciphers employed in their Puranic counting were, however, there but in a different, though striking pertinent, context: the names belonged to the different throws of dice gambling, and the ciphers corresponded to the number of verses or mantras contained in the Rig Veda alone, or in the Sama and Yajur combined.[3] However, when they developed in a rather systematised manner from the Epics down to the Puranas, wherefrom they were properly developed and astronomically justified by the astronomers and astrologers of the times (*jotisas*), these Yugas too were adjusted to the 3+1 model, and the +1, applied to the current era, became the measure unit to be projected by its multiples on the other preceding three dimensions. These, then, become the double, triple and fourfold of the basic era, giving to the whole the completeness of the +1 at the 10th degree. Philosophically, that figure representing Time has also its parallel in the aspect attributed to the Absolute in the form of the Cosmic Man, Maha Purusha, whose lower fourth is the visible part of the Universe while the other three fourths remain inaccessible and transcendent. Mythologically, the whole cycle is connected with the world of Vishnu, and the whole cycle is considered to be equivalent to a day and a night in the world of Brahma, the Creator, issued from the sleeping Main Divinity.

The involved actual ciphers begin with a starting unit which is probably reckoned according to a 'sexagesimal' system (a fact that gave some scholars the idea of a first influence from Babylonian culture and its advanced astronomical science, where counting was made around the main figure of sixty) applied to the sun, as passing through the Zodiacal houses and with an eye on the phenomenon called "the precession of Equinoxes"; such a unit is the length value ascribed to our current era, the Kali Yuga and is usually of 432,000 years. The total result is the following:

1. Krita Yuga
   Equal to 1,728,000 years == 4x432,000

2. Tetra Yuga
   Equal to 1,296,000 years == 3x432,000

3. Dvapara Yuga
   Equal to 864,000 years == 2x432,000

4. Kali Yuga
   Equal to 432,000 years == 1x432,000

Our actual era:
Together they form the Maha Yuga of 4,320,000 years == 10x432,000.

As already hinted at, this rather long stretch of time is but one day in the life of the Creator at the end of which, through an impressive catastrophe reminding us of Tropical storms with bursts of lightening and powerful inundations bringing about total destruction, the whole cosmos is dissolved—including its Gods and Goddesses—into a dark Night of equal length. During this period Vishnu, the only remaining being together with the cosmic Serpent Sesha, sleeps afloat the all-covering cosmic Waters recumbent on the coils of that very serpent. Sometimes He dreams. The next dawn starts with some waves in those waters, through some stirring of heated energy which, in the ancient Brahmanic vision coagulated itself into a Unit and then into a cosmic Egg, and in the Pauranic mythology of Vishnuitic saga grows as a lotus flower from the *nabhi*, the navel, of the main resting God. On this lotus sits the above mentioned Creator ready to stir up his heating energy (*tapas*) and to start all over again for another long day, another Maha Yuga. Later, in an advanced Puranic tradition, the tendency of elongating more and more such an account went out of hand and the Mahayugas were grouped in further clusters of 1000 into a Kalpa, which took over the dimension of a day of Brahma(n) over against another equal stretch of Kalpa forming the night. Every day-night measure then was inserted in the 'Life' of Brahma(n) extending to the ideal (human) length of 100 years (but, of course, in Divine years when concerning the main Creator). This more than 'astronomical' length was also subjected to an ulterior addiction in Manvantaras, each formed by 71.000 Mahayugas, thus making 14 Manvantaras in a Kalpa. In this way humanity, though belonging to the last portion of a Mahayuga, could gain again its central position in the wheel of Time by being placed at the end of the Seventh Manvantara, the current one under the auspices of the Seventh Manu, Vaivantara? Useless to say that the traditional astronomers had hard work to do in order to try to match the various traditions and ciphers together and with proper astronomical data.[4] Each period, or sub-period in this counting, is threatened by annihilation through a violent End of the World (Pralaya) marking the entrance of the night or of the death of the Creator previous to a new day or a new life to come.

Likely, the meaning hidden behind these high numbers is an attempt to insert the various communities and their individual members into an ordained whole including not only space but also time, yet without loosing the infinite perspective of that Eternity and of that Immensity hovering over Reality. The advantage of this vision is that at any moment one may be able to orient oneself by knowing one's own place in the flowing of yearly revolutions, or even of Yugas' revolutions, and, at the same time, cannot be compelled and pushed on by the hopeless feeling of 'pressing time' leaving no open chances once some of them have been missed in the rushing on of hours, days and years. The Yugas reckoning, spreading in slow recurrent waves, conforms with the cyclical rhythms of a convulsive but repetitious Nature allowing people and nations to recover lost opportunities and to grow through progressions as well as regressions toward any improvement, or impoverishment, of material, social and religious conditions till the point when a maturity of spiritual detachment is at last reached. At this moment nothing really matters any longer for the person so grown up and both Yugas and social position appear for what they actually were all along: crafty or masterful ways of systematizing an originally chaotically cluster of perceptions enhanced by a too large and too full tropical land but without any real substance behind them. We shall come back to this while dealing with religion and its world-vision. Meanwhile we seize here the opportunity to consider the disturbing lack of historical sense often remarked upon regarding Indian cultures (at least disturbing for the Westerners who are such masters of history that they cannot even conceive a different valuation of time).

b. Sense of history

After what has been seen up to now, it should not be too difficult to realize why Indians generally resist the urge of lining up the major events of their 'history' in a straight string so as to prevent them overlapping. Most of the people living in more temperate climates, with more reliable seasonal recurrences, have the leisure of measuring a not destructive time; and this allows a proper planning of the future, even a distant one. And, with the mastering of one's future, one's past stands up like a reflection in a mirror with all its meaningful backward sequence. In this way, past and future are blended into a harmonious whole mirroring one another so that 'historical' facts can be accordingly arranged. Greeks, Romans, Hebrews, Chinese, Egyptians and perhaps Etruscans too, cared to note down in well constructed chronicles the most salient and important events of their nations' life so that these may be dated and therefore get differentiated and duly classified. Indians, instead, at every change of season are dazzled and amazed by finding themselves still alive—while this would not always be the case for their less lucky neighbours—and they look out for the next change with a deep-rooted sense of insecurity. Thus, if the future is uncertain it does not offer the possibility of having a mirror to reflect and therefore to value the past. All energies of the inhabitants of this inhospitable country are concentrated on the present, which appears hard enough for leaving almost no leisure for anything else; a present that absorbs automatically its past, somehow sieved and selected in its more significant moments for individuals and communities, and its future, which becomes essentially a chance full of new risks. In this way, the actual moment appears to be built up on roots deeply inserted in the actions previously performed and these are, in their turn, projected forward to include those still to come, which are but the unavoidable outcome of the actions and events of past and present alike. The whole process has been philosophically elaborated under the well-defined "Law of Karma", which shall be discussed later on.

However, to live in the present, if it is a highly desirable preparation for developing the spiritual dimension, it is less propitious or even suitable for measuring time according to a linear arrangement of dateable events. When the past is lived only for what valuables can carry into the actual moment and future is thinkable only as a suitable receptacle for the effects attached to certain significant actions already performed, there is not much scope for anything else but for 'today' (in the Hindi language: *aaj*) thus depriving of meaning the other two temporal dimensions: the yesterdays and tomorrows, significantly expressed in Hindi by the same term: *kal*, from the Sanskrit *Kaala* meaning Time in general. That is why it is sometimes so difficult to sort out the different layers of Indian historical events, especially when dealing with faraway periods now woven into mythically significant teachings and cultural landmarks, all presented in the same texts without concern for possible later additions or amendments. Even at a personal level a too strong concentration on the actual moment can be experienced as a loss of differentiation between one day and another, while the few eventful happenings tend to overlap in recollection just rendering dating a kind of a problem. And, if this can be noticed at the level of individuals, with more grounds can be applied to social conditions where the significant moments scattered along various periods are integrated into tradition and proposed again as a homogeneous whole in the heritage of a religion that, if on one side can be said to have closed the central nucleus of its 'revelation'—its myths and its traditional science—like most religions of the world; on the other is still open to new interpretations and modifications brought about by its "technicians of the sacred" (to use a term employed by Mircea Eliade): the brahmins, on one side, as responsible performers of rites and preservers of sacred texts and the realized spiritual persons, on the other, as legitimate innovators of the same on the ground of having acquired the inner authority for interpreting, adding and rearranging tradition as such[5]. We shall return to them when discussing the role played by such people in the preservation and continuation of their culture.[6]

NOTES

1. In Autumnal Equinox there are the big Festivities of the first nine- days of the New Moon of Asvina Month (more of less between middle of September and middle of October) with its culmination in the festival of Lights, called Di(pa)wali, at the following New Moon Day. In the spring there is Vasant Panchami (the Fifth Day of the New Moon in spring (February)), and, already advanced in the heat, the Nine day of March- April New Moon with its culmination at Midday of the Ninth with the celebration of Ram's Birthday. Krishan's Birth falls, instead, in the middle of Rainy Season, at Midnight of the dark- quarter Moon of Bhadrapada. The Solstice has its culmination in the new start of the Sun toward North, at Makar Sankranti the 14th of January. The summer one has no special emphasis. Ch. 3.a.ü

2. See. e.g. the Sundays dedicated to the Sun-God; Mondays to Shiva; Tuesdays and Saturdays for Hanuman; and so on. In the moon-cycle, the dark- half moon is for Ganesh; the night before the New Moon is for Shiva, etc.

3. See the equivalences in the exhaustive study of L.G. Reimann, *Tiemp ciclico y eras del Mundo en la India*, Mexico City, 1989, pp. 55 ff.

4. For a complete survey, comments and parallels with other cultures see, beside the quoted work of Riemann, also E.G. McClain, *The Myth of Invariance, the Origin of the Gods, Mathematics and Music from the Rig-Veda to Plato*, NY (N. Hays)1976, esp. ch VII

5. For a complete survey, comments and parallels with other cultures see, beside the quoted work of Riemann, also E.G. McClain, *The Myth of Invariance, the Origin of the Gods, Mathematics and Music from the Rig-Veda to Plato*, NY (N.Hays)1976, esp. ch VII

6. For a reflection about this continuing creations of Indian culture see Brian K. Smith, *Reflections on Resemblance, Ritual and Religion*, Delhi (Motilal)1998 (org. 1989) especially ch. 1& 2

CHAPTER 4
Coordinates For Individual Persons

The scheme of 3+1 followed for settling nature, society and even Time into a workable unity in full respect of their multiplicity and multiformity is kept also at the level of individuals' life. Differing from the rather general trend of Theistic nations holding together their subjects into a compact society—like the members of a polis, of a civitas, of a kingdom for the sake and in behalf of whose as a whole either the king or the State's representatives performed and offered sacrifice as a common action—Indian society, notwithstanding the great emphasis bestowed on togetherness in joint families, village unity, caste solidarity and the like, has a particular regard for its individual members and lavishes on them its keenest concern for their proper physical, religious and spiritual health and growth. It is perhaps for this reason that proclivity for compartmentalizing whatever is thought as inherently only too inclined to grow wildly if not properly checked, has directed Vedic culture, through the alertness of its philosophers and theologians, to come also upon individuals to help them crossing the different stages of life by making them aware that their existence too consisted of steps (made out of ashramas) to be consciously attained and passed through; and also to put square in front of them the aims (artha) they should pursue in order to maintain themselves whilst on the righteous path without frustrations and in full respect of their respective social duties. However, in order to prevent egocentrism, often the outcome of too much stress on individuality, Brahmanism devised the theory of binding each individual to society and cosmic order through the theory of Debts (rina), according to which every person is conceived as born with four types of obligations towards their Gods, Rishis, Ancestors, and fellow beings. Yet, in order to give a well-founded reason to the discrimination established by their compartmentalised social body and culture, every person was laden with an allotted 'destiny' based not on whimsical fate but grounded on previous deeds according to a well-elaborated Law of Karman.

a. Age of Life (Ashramas)

The first of these divisions, called in Sanskrit *'ashramas'*, considers the natural steps of human life in its physiological growth, maturity and decay as different stages that have to be crossed and passed through[1]. Such a division manages at the same time to conform as well to the above-mentioned scheme of four, taken in its sum of 3+1. Thus, after first childhood, which is not counted because the infant is still part of its parents' personality, the little boy enters in what is considered to be the first degree of his career, namely that of the Student, (Brahmacharin). The entrance in such a stage generally was marked by a special ceremony in which the boy was formally removed from his family milieu and entrusted to a teacher. This person, in receiving his pupil, symbolically incorporated him, like a mother, as an embryo and then accepted him into his household, usually a hermitage in the forest or wilderness outside villages, to live together with his own wife and children. He imparted to him his knowledge of the sacred texts and in general religious and cultural tradition, beginning with a sacred formula to be repeated as an initiatory task. As a counterpart the child had to obey, respect and serve his teacher and his family, while strictly maintaining the laws of purity especially that of chastity—this injunction becoming very important during late adolescence not only as a valuable means of self-control and asceticism, but also as a protection for the female folk of the teachers' household. It is perhaps as a reminiscence of this traditional system that even in modern types of education there is a marked preference for boarding schools and university hostels, while the initiatory ceremony is still kept as a "sacrament" (*samskara*). The girls, instead, generally received their education in domestic duties either at home under the supervision of their mothers or directly in their in-laws house in case of child marriage. However, in Vedic times it can be inferred from some sacred texts and Greek classical references that women were not banned from traditional learning and philosophical debates ("provided they are not the head-guru's own wives and daughters" says Strabo.[2]

This first period ends with a new ceremony generally concluding with the marriage of the ex-'boy' now an adult and ready to enter into his second stage, that of head of family, (*Grihasta*), with all its social responsibilities toward wife, children, family life, work and, in ancient times and still among orthodox ones, especially ritual duties—domestic rites, of course, because only a very meagre portion of even those entitled to perform solemn sacrifices actually got engaged in them; anyway, if by any chance they belong to those few, it is in this very group of age that they can do it. This, in fact, is the stage in which a responsible man enkindles his own sacred fire (the domestic one started by his marriage), which has to stay with him all through his active life. If he decides not to retire from active life or if he happens to die while still in his maturity, it is officially that fire which would be brought to the cremation ground to perform his last offering, that of his body on the funeral pyre, at the hand of his proxy, i.e., his son. Had he to decide otherwise and to follow the prescriptions of the Ashramas to the letter, once he reaches the threshold of old age, an individual had the choice either to retire to a secluded place, generally a dwelling in the wilderness, or to wander in the forest or from monastery to monastery (ashrams), alone or together with his faithful wife—if she agrees to follow him. By this, then, he enters in the third stage, that of Vanaprastha (a Sanskrit compound noun whose first term means "forest"). In this he still retains his fire, therefore he is not totally free from ritual work, but domestic rites are certainly simplified in so far as he burns in it wild rice and forest food. He uses the rest of his free time in pursuing ascetic disciplines, studying the philosophy behind the sacred texts and slowly detaching himself from the needs and attachments acquired during his active engagement in the everyday world.

However, though formally no longer in the whirl of life and competition for survival, those belonging to this third stage of life are somehow still on the side of the 3 of the quaternitas, meaning that they somehow still belong to this side of the world even if on their way out of it. In this respect it is only the fourth stage, which definitely forms the +1 of the scheme. This is the stage of the total Renunciation (Samnyasa) in which the Renouncer (samnyasin) has entirely and definitely left the level of worldly involvement to enter into a new and different dimension where all cultural, social and religious constructions are left behind together with human concerns and worries. He enters in it through another ceremony in which, among other symbolic acts, he "swallows" or interiorize his fire, after having used it for the last time in his funeral ceremonies performed on himself by himself, thus liberating his son from such a duty. If his wife does not follow him into his retirement, when her time would be ripe she would be cremated with the fire of her son as if a widow. Then, being now completely free from ritualistic practices, the samnyasi meditates upon them, lives them in his heart till becoming identified with them and with the Deity he had chosen as his Ishta Devata, the God of his preference, till a moment will come in which he is, in a certain sense, so innerly fortified that he can be considered fit to directly face the scaring Void opening like an abyss on the obscure depths of Infinity, of Eternity, in a word of the impersonal Absolute, One without a second. Being, then, so to say "at home" with such a Source of everything, the Samnyasi, having become a sage, is—as we are going to see towards the end of this presentation—in the position of entirely mastering the Sacred Knowledge[3] and therefore able to grasp its inner meaning so as to interpret it again for the people of his era even to the point of modifying and adding to the lot. Officially, then, he should belong to those very few who have reached liberation even during their life-time and therefore have ceased to struggle for detachment, for mastering the self, because they have attained inner peace and joy or rather serenity; and if ever he is still found near temples, especially while begging for food, he does no longer need the psychological support of idols' presence either in places or in images.

Practically, however, the stage of Samnyasa is today almost equalised with that of monks (usually called sadhus, swamis, Babas, not as common designations but as titles of respect and appreciation for the category) and both the groups fall into a category which includes all sorts of spiritual seekers even if they are still far away from perfection and often have a long way to go in this direction. This happens through the sheer necessity of adjusting the rules to practical situations. In everyday life, the previous step of Vanaprastha has almost fallen out of fashion: are wives seldom inclined to follow their husbands in such an enterprise, and even for men the fact of remaining on the thresholds of ritual duties does not suit their quest for inner freedom. Besides, along with elderly people who got tired of their spent life, there are a lot of younger ones—and they are by far more numerous than suspected to be—who feel the attraction of spiritual enlightenment right from early age so that they, as at all were raised as Brahmacharins, tend to jump directly from the first to the last stage, without lingering in between. Too young and disinterested in family life as to go through all the prescribed stages (or, simply in order to escape an unpleasant arranged marriage) they go straight to some masters (gurus) to be initiated into the renounces' path, which ipso facto becomes a path of learning as well as struggling toward that perfection so hard to attain.

Anyway, this last stage, the +1, allows man to plunge into a Spiritual dimension of existence from whatever age and from whatever situation, caste and stage of life he happens to belong to. Here, in fact, every conditioning element (be it social or religious) is left behind together with the feeling of belonging to a family, a caste or a nation. The "monk" is really a "solitary" one and his individuality is absolute —without, however, this being a hindrance if it happens to him to become a guru surrounded by a variable number of disciples, devotees and common people seeking help, blessings and wisdom from them, as the case arises for a few of them.[4]

b. Aims of life (purushartha)

Often, in those generalizations so easily applied to all religions by enhancing one among their many points (for instance: Christianity is considered the religion of Love and Social Solidarity; Buddhism that of Compassion and Illumination; Confucianism of High Morality and so on), Hinduism has been labeled as the Spirituality of Liberation and its followers taken as a whole as a bunch of dreamers and idealists little concerned with this phenomenal world—and thus deemed as responsible for the 'backward' conditions prevalent in the country (backward, of course, when judged with the metre of Westernized modern mentality...). Seen, however, in a closer way, nothing seems to be more unjust that this statement. Already in what has been shown so far, it transpires a diffused interest combined with worry, for the well being of people and societies living in this very world and busy with their own welfare and with improving their material, physical and cultural conditions. All those religious activities engaged in providing Nature with Order and points of reference, all those efforts bestowed on the theory of dividing but in unity and of unifying while respecting diversity, were all intended for rendering *this* world liveable at all possible levels and degrees, even when assigning duties and rights to different human groups in their various capacities, stretched as well to cover the distinctive features of physiological ages.

A further step in this positive and mundane World-view is represented by the concept of purusartha, or the aims or tasks or purposes of men in life. These Arthas, these purposes, too are presented according to the usual scheme of 3+1 (that some classical texts sometimes propose in the variation of 2+2 module) and of these only the last, the +1, is placed radically out of the solid grasp of human social life and interests. The main bulk of the three of them relates with aims well rooted in worldly necessities, enhancing and properly directing the legitimate aspirations of those who care for welfare and survival of worldly existence. These aims are, in their increasing order: Kama, or Desire—for procreation, for better life; Artha, or Interest—for wealth, career, position, power; Dharma, or Order, in its Religious, Political and Social aspects and implications. This third aim, however, is on a slightly different plan with respect to the other two, and this is the reason why some texts prefer to disconnect it from the main worldly aims and approaching it, instead, to the +1: i.e. Moksa or Liberation(1). Actually, Dharma is rather an enveloping attitude than a proper aim in itself; it is what puts a restrain to an inordinate and immoderate use of the other two, thus avoiding subscribing to potentially licentious behaviours. For the rest, if properly handled, Desire and Interest are the foundations of social growth in individuals as well as in groups and form the springboard for a natural urge of improvement and progress.[5]

There are classical treatises dealing with these 'worldly' aims, exalting their respective properties and pointing out the best manners to display the related skills for attaining the best results in their pursuit. The Kamasutra is the most well known composition of this kind; here sensual and sexual desires are displayed in all subtleties for extracting maximum of pleasure, yet Dharma should be present as a higher purpose in order to avoid excesses and above all as a way of inserting a superior meaning to a mere enjoyment. Obviously Kamas's aim is oriented toward procreation, thus directed toward increasing population and acquiring affection and, therefore, attachments, that is to say toward strengthening ties with worldly life.

The same can be said of the Arthasastra, the treatise concerned with the attainment of wealth, position, and power. It is a text addressed primarily to a king, the one involved in the welfare not only of himself and his family but of all his subjects; nonetheless any person engaged in pursuing wealth and career, or in improving his social conditions, can extract useful advises from it. Also the range of this text is clearly within the scope of this world and its attention is concentrated in giving directions for endorsing a better standard in life, regardless of religious purposes except in the sense of keeping oneself within the boundaries of Dharma (Order, Justice, also strongly belonging to this concrete side of Reality).

And, as a matter of fact, even Dharma can be in its turn also one aspect, one aim, in itself; it is the aim that Brahmacharins and Brahmins propose to themselves in the same manner as people engaged in fulfilling earthly tasks put their heart in the strive for attaining perfection in the pursuit of love and wealth. After all a traditional student is trained to learn the texts and the items pertaining to the Vedas, which are the perceptible form of Dharma, while Brahmins keeping in line with their traditional duties are engaged in protecting, maintaining and transmitting Dharma, through the recitation, interpretation, and occasionally direct ritualistic performance, of Vedic texts and culture. However, Dharma, as seen before, is also the

Order, the Rule, overlooking the whole cultural display. It is the natural heir of the Vedic Rita at the time in which a different ritual order comes to the surface, in a shift to a more 'popular' and widespread form of cult.

This brings us to another point in the intricacies of such Brahmanical world-view: everything we have presented so far is strictly interconnected. As it could be inferred while analyzing the Purusharthas, each aim can be properly applied to a category of people in the caste-system and to the age group in which one happens to be at the moment. Thus, Dharma is the concern and aim of the Brahmans as a category and of the students of the three main castes in their youth. Kama and Artha, in various degrees, apply to the adults in the full blooming of their worldly engagements, the Grihasta or Pater-familias, especially those belonging to the second and third groups of castes, because Desire is the driving force behind the instinct (and social duty) of procreation and behind the strive for power (the Warriors and Kings) and richness (the Traders); while Artha, Interest, is sought for by both of them in order to sharpen the skill for obtaining enjoyment and welfare. Thus, castes, ages, aims, all conform to one another in a harmony which integrates into a whole the various aspects of this tropical exuberance embedding in a proper Order its multiple tassels as in a gigantic three-dimensional jig-saw puzzle, where also Time enters in the game through its well allotted Festivals and also its theoretical assignment of Yugas. The actual Kali Yuga, being the one where disorder prevails, belongs to the caste of Sudras, so that it does not come as a surprise the raise into political and economical power of members of the lower classes with their thirst of revenge and subversion of traditional hierarchy. When, in the next chapter, we shall discuss the religious dimension with its rituals, sacred texts and the various aspects of Gods and Goddesses, and then we shall be in the position to add or insert also the religious realm into the spectrum so far presented.

The fourth aim, just merely mentioned above, is *moksha*, the "desire for liberation (*mukti*)" and falls out of the group of the main 3. because it stands for a total jump into the "Other" the spiritual dimension where all worldly aims and differentiations are overcome. As such it pertains to the fourth stage of life.

c. Sacraments (Samskaras)

Samskaras, as stated, accompany man through his main steps in life, underlining natural changes—thus subtracting them from Nature in order to insert them in a cultural pattern—and helping such changes to be charged with all the required energy necessary for impressing themselves on the awareness of the subjects undergoing them.[6] The 'coming to age' is stressed in the ceremony called 'upasana' or 'yajnapavitra'[7] janu in which the boy leaves infancy and takes on the "sacred thread", symbol of the duties assumed with adult age: especially, he is given his personal Mantra for its dutiful repetition as ritual assignment. Among Brahmins this ceremony takes place around the age of twelve or fourteen years thus making the youth fit for learning the Sacred Texts; among the members of the other two main castes entitled to the ceremony, the same takes place just before marriage, taking up in this way its proper role of marking the entrance to adulthood in preparation to the main step of heading a family. If in the common practice of a joint-family his authority in the house is somewhat dwarfed by his father who officially remains the head of the household till his death or till his retirement to the forest (or out of family-business) this does not hinder the fact that as a master of his own fire the newly initiated and married man has his sway on his own small group.

Marriage is then the second step in life's growth and is by far the most important event for both the members of the couple.[8] For women, especially, it introduces a major change in their existence, entailing as it is a shift from their birthplace to their in-laws residence and way of life. Often she is very young and her main task, before begetting a child of her own, is that of serving her in-law parents, while considering her husband as her god. As far as the ceremony is concerned, it takes place either in an open space in the courtyard of the bride's house or somewhere nearby it always in the open, under a huge tent to protect the guests from the weather. Such ceremony varies according to regions and to castes, sometimes also according to special traditions in special groups inside the same caste, so that it is very difficult to cover all variations in a single short description. The main unfailing item present in all marriages, however, is Fire, the newly enkindled fire of the new couple, the one that will receive the couple's offerings, beginning from the first one in the marriage ceremony itself down to everyday domestic rites. Round this Fire, taken as witness, the couple walks in pradakshina (circumambulation of something giving it one's right) once, thrice or seven times according to local and 'castal' customs. Many of the ritual features and meanings in the ceremony point at the fact that marriage was regarded as a happening concerning adulthood thus ruling out the later custom of child marriage, very common throughout the whole country till a few decades ago and still popular in villages and among many strata of the society. This practice, grown in years, became somewhat a habit for convenient reasons of various kind; and this, at its turn, brought with it some adjustments in the cultural behaviour, such as a split, ranging from some days or months to even years, between the actual wedding ceremony and the transference of the young bride to her husband's and in-laws' home, which amounts to be a good procedure in so far as it allows two people till then perfect strangers to one another (the marriages, at those times as well as today, being arranged by parents without the youngsters concerned having ever seen each other) to come to know themselves better, but can be also turned to a bad one if the *vidayi* (as the definitive departure from the paternal house is called) would mean a surplus in the dowry system or, as it had happened in rare cases, the groom did not accept the grown up bride. In ancient times, up to rather recently, marriage ceremonies used to cover a period of a few days and involved a huge amount of expenditure. Now, because of modern lack of avalaible time and also in an attempt to reduce at least a little bit of the still very high expenses, everything is generally shrunk into one night or half a day.

When the child is expected and then born, especially if he is a boy (but also girls have their own ceremonies) other ceremonies are involved, which are prolonged during the first months and years of the child's life, marking the moment of coming into this world with the purifications of the mother required to atone for blood pollution, continuing with the imposition of name, with the ministration of the first solid food, the solemnity celebrating the coming out of the first tooth, and so on and so forth, including the main ceremony of cutting the hair the child wore at its birth (for the boy this cut is delayed between his first to his fifth year of life; for the girl it can be celebrated from her eighth month to her first year). All these ceremonies are performed under the aegis of father authority and father fire, when fire is required, with the help of the family priest (Purohita) or a professional just hired for the occasion.[9]

The next ceremony an adult may submit himself to is the optional retirement (now practically becoming obsolete) into the third stage of life, or the more common and still retained practice of directly entering in the fourth stage, that of samnyasa or monk. It is also called "taking initiation" (diksa) into monkhood, and also varies according to the institution or sect (sampradaya) to which either the guru or the aspirant monk belongs. The main stress, whatever tradition is followed, is given to the moment of cutting the ties binding the novice to his everyday world, including his family affection and caste's duties, as a preliminary stage for assuming a new identity into a new birth. What all this entails shall be seen in the fourth part of this work, when the spiritual path of individuals shall be considered. Here the ritual aspect of the matter will be sketched out, presenting the feature of a veritable death—if the ceremony is performed for a retiring householder this one is supposed even to perform his funerals officiating as the main performer in the place of his son who is exempted from such office when the right time would come; followed by a rebirth into a new 'unconditioned' condition. Since, according to the various degrees in life's curriculum the last step toward liberation is supposed to be taken from a Brahman position, some of the previous ceremonies performed over a 'novice' belonging to another caste have the purpose of gradually letting him pass through all the degrees intervening from the caste of his birth up to Brahman hood, with the aim of finally throwing away everything connecting him with his cultural world. For the sake of undergoing the full ceremony a guru is required, who is the initiator and who gives the neophit his spiritual task and his initiatory mantra. Where there is no guru, the sadhu-to-be can dispense with external performances and may set out into his new chosen life without rituals or even without an inner change of heart—a not too rare a case, as a matter of fact.[10]

The last 'sacrament' is the one performed on the dead body of the deceased.[11] Officially it is connected with sacrifice and the body itself is the main offering. It is performed, traditionally, with the household fire of the pater-familias, which was meant for his wife and himself. Today, at least in Benares and possibly in some other holy cities, it is purchased in a special place near the burning ground from special people in charge of the whole rite, but occasionally it can also be kindled on the spot where the pyre has been erected. If the wife dies before her husband, the latter being the master of his fire, enkindled her pyre, but if he precedes her, she will remain in charge of her son who uses his own fire for it (today the involvement of the nearer relation, either father, husband or son, is in the purchasing of fire and enkindling the pyre, since there is no longer a well kept fire in the hearth of the house). For a householder the performer is the son (that is why having a son is so important for a Hindu); and for a young fellow is his father (if still alive) or his brother. Children not eligible to have had their own fire yet and before the ceremony of yajnapavitra or upayana, are not cremated but either burried or, when it is possible, composed on a big stone and thrown into a sacred river. Not entitled to cremation were also the sadhus and sanyasas whose funerals had been already ritually performed, after which their very fire has been interiorized during their initiation to monkhood; and also the holders of particularly impure diseases? Since the main philosophy behind cremation, after the change in philosophical doctrine over the value of life which occurred at the time of the Upanishads, is that Fire, instead of "cooking to perfection" the body so as to transform it into an immortal entity, helps in dissolving its main elements into their cosmic counterparts, a polluted 'fuel' is bound to spread polluted elements into the whole universe in its five main components: earth, water, fire, air, ether.

The main bulk of verses recited during each and all these "Sacraments" is mostly taken from the Vedic mantras, though also Puranic and Epic verses can be included.[12]

The Samskaras, in their function of marking life as a punctuation or of fixing it with special knots in weaving individual realities, were soon so much intertwined with Hindu culture in general that the word also helds the more generic meaning of "life situation", "position in society..."[13]

d. The doctrine of Debts, Rina.

But, as already hinted at previously, too much concern for the individual could make him to forget, or at least overlook even to the point of ignoring it, the importance of one's place in the world and society, with all its complex chain of relationships. Brahmanism could not let it pass without trying to put a remedy to it. It was already bad enough—from its organizational point of view—the conquered freedom attained by the members of the fourth stage of life and by the monks or sadhus, for allowing such feeling to spread unchecked. Their 'remedy' for such danger is known as the theory of Debt, RINA. The name comes from the Vedic times and designates the act of taking something from somebody with the obligation to give it back (with or without interest)[14], but here it is employed in a wider and more encompassing sense also involving a feeling of sin and culpability. This theory can be seen as a consequence of, or rather the perfecting touch in building up the bulk of rules aroused in the huge task of re-setting again life after the transition from a nomadic existence carried on by a rather homogeneous society, to a well articulated civilization, requiring, as seen, many social levels that had to be well distinguished but at the same time firmly interconnected to one another so as to form a well-knitted unity. In this theory, man is conceived as being born as a Debt, or, putting it differently, to have an inborn dept imposed on him at the moment of his coming into this world. This dept (rina) consists of three (or, according to a variant in the tradition, four) obligations, which he has to rescue himself from in the course of his life: those contracted toward his Gods, toward the Seers of his culture, toward his Ancestors and, if added to the account, toward his fellow-beings.[15] This could also be seen as a strong and effective device to prevent untimely shrinking from one's duties toward society—past, present and future—and in this respect they are as well related with the stages and aims of life just discussed.

According to this theory, man has also to be furnished with adequate means to acquit himself from such bonds. Such means are provided by right behaviour and especially by rites, some of which are open to everybody while others are restricted to the caste members. This, however, is not a tragedy or an injustice (as contested by some scholars) because, though the idea of Rina theoretically apply to every human being, in practice it refers only to the people sharing the basic tenets of this Sanskrit culture; the Sudras, and even more the tribals, have their own ways which, in any case, are much easier and less burdensome. Be it as it may, by the very act of being born, a child, especially if the elder son, frees his father from the debt contracted with his Ancestors by assuming them over himself, together with the others in which his father was socially and religiously involved; and he begins to redeem himself from the debts due to the Seers by learning the Vedas as soon as he comes to the age of receiving initiation into the first stage of life: Brahmacharin. At his turn, at the time of marriage at the entrance in the second stage, that of the Householder, the individual is ready to beget his own son on whom to pass over the chain of debts and at the same time is in the position to acquire his domestic fire on which to perform his daily rites toward the Gods, thus acquitting himself and his wife from his Rina with respect to them. As Householder he is also in the position to pay back his due to his fellow-beings as well by feeding them as honoured guests whenever they show up as unexpected strangers, beggars or friends, thus ensuring a kind of solidarity between human beings. Another effect of this theory is that of reinforcing the ties linking one person with his culture, his past and his future in a country where, as it has been seen, the overwhelming difficulties of the present do not leave proper chances for a linear counting of time as implied in historical conceptions.

In other words, an enforced mutual sense of hospitality may be interpreted also as a debt contracted with one's own generation and tbus extended to ensure a sense of solidarity between all its members even beyond the boundaries of one's village or community, in the present; while the begetting of a son, besides guaranteeing a continuation in the future with an unbroken link, is also seen as a powerful mean to tightening up the link with the past not only of the individuals but of the entire society, since a son is a debt paid to ancestors. In its turn, the fulfilment of the Debt supposedly incurred toward the Rishis is an important move for assuring a perpetuation of Vedic culture, through transmitting it by heart from generation to generation. Without this commitment imposed to the selected members of the proper castes, especially the Brahmins, chances would have been that the powerful inheritance of the Vedas, with all its various branches and literature, would have been lost long time back, when that knowledge was made available to a much wider range of population in the form of Epics and Purana's mythology as shall be seen later. Though this later literature has assured the continuation and transmission of its basic ideas and beliefs, the learning and recitation of the ancient hymns, with their exegetical Corpus, served to keep alive in a direct way the cultural and religious efforts of the ancient Seers, just remaining a force connecting in a single act the past with the future in the solid moment of the present, not only on a physiological level, but on the more important ground of a common civilization. In the same manner, Worship, the main feature of every religion, is assured (and this assurance becomes essential in the light of the promised individual freedom of the 'realized' persons, the final and coveted aim of the members of the fourth stage of life: samnyasa) when presented as an unavoidable rescue from one's Debt to the Gods. Such Rina, though appearing at a first glance as so obvious as not to be worthy a second thought, can be considered one of the most essential factors in the preservation of Brahmanic religion and culture because, in the changing moods over the millennia with the Yajna performances in constant decline and the figures of the Gods themselves changing shape and character in accordance with their 'mythical' presentation by Pauranic and Epical bards and sages, rites and rituals could rather have easily been dispensed with (like in the case of the seekers for direct freedom and realization) or simplified to the extreme.[16]

Yet, even in spite of the ancient Sages' concern, in the work of spiritually minded philosophers soon this Debt towards the various Deities was 'exposed' for what it really stood: the Debt that all human beings (or, for that matter, all beings as such) have finally to pay at the end of their life: that due to Death. We have reached here the actual main concern common to all religions and to humanity as such: the puzzling and somehow always unexpected event of Death suddenly cutting into every living thing. Death, the great mystery, which should not have a place in a well constructed life, but which eventually claims its due regardless of knowledge, health and power. Death is so unwelcome to humanity that in almost all religions and cultures of the world (including the ultra-modern atheists, scientists and communists who try to assure themselves that eventually science and advanced medicine will get human beings rid of it) that it is conceived as not belonging to human destiny as such. It is said, in fact, by various different myths in all religions that originally it did not belong to human life, but was inevitably brought in by a primordial event either drawn on by a mistake or by the cunning behaviour of some 'supernatural' or even 'natural' being.[17] In India, however, except perhaps in some lost myths hinted upon in some hymns to the Asvins reminding us of a similar instance in ancient Greece in the case of Demeter where Death could be kept off by special rites. Death is so violent and obviously present that it does not seem to have been ever conceived as absent from any period, not even in a lost mythical past. Actually Death is so important in this Tropical country that it is conceived as the first-born of the Absolute[18] and is so powerful that threatens even the Main Creator[19]. However, Indian man is not immune from the common desire of keeping on living for ever, so, in a more practical way than many others, he challenges his unavoidable end by seeking immortality through a proper ransom from Yama, the King of the dead, in the form of appropriate rites. This means that, in this conception as a debt to the Gods, this ransom from Yama is extended to include all possible types of worship, thus incorporating again at a different level the ancient position of Yajnas and other classical rites.

e. Conception of Death

Though in a way that seems, perhaps, to interrupt a well planned mandala, the Indian conception of Death have to be included as a kind of 'fifth layer' at the end of this chapter devoted to the appropriate building up of individuals, both in their single personality and in their social body. However, even in this case we keep in line with Vedic tradition because the number five too has its own sacrality, in so far as, according to the texts, the (Indian) seasons are also five, together with the main directions which can as well be intended to reach that cipher by adding the Zenit to the four corners, while even the rites comply with this different order or organization by including a 'fifth layer' in the piling up of a special Fire-altar during a Soma Sacrifice. Death, in fact, is but the crowning of individual lives, it is what gives the final meaning of every existence, and at the same time is the threat which interrupts or puts a definitive end, according to different beliefs and cultural situations, to every human enterprise. It is, in a way, something that has to be reckoned with, no matter how great, powerful, confident or healthy a person is supposed to be. Not for nothing the main final debt, Rina, man is called to pay is that due to his unavoidable End. Yet, the very fact that a debt can be paid and the debtor rescued to freedom, leaves open a hope for survival, which Indian thought is called upon to define in a way or another either as a form of after-life, or in a more spiritual mode of existence.

Concern for death is, in any case, a common issue for all humanity and all religions of the world deal with it in a manner or another since all over the planet man refuses to accept his mortal destiny. Most of the time, however, such longing for immortality is seen—by the majority of mythologies—as a lost possibility, regarded with an immense nostalgia and regret over an opportunity gone for ever...except in the case of a few privileged people, like heroes or the members of special religious and spiritual societies. The case of Greek Mysteries is among the first to come into mind. Myths of all kind and cultures are unanimously agreeing that "at the beginning", that is to say: before actual 'historical' times started, men and Gods were sharing the same conditions of immortality till 'something' unfortunate happened to change such ideal situation: either an unwanted mistake, or a wilfully cunning behaviour, or a straight forward sin, so that Death came in as a result of it. The story of Adam is the most known case in point, and the same can be said of the Greek Myth of Prometheus with his cunning partition in the respective shares of Sacrificial portions or of the thousand tales of the so called 'primitives' where either an animal or a trickster of some sort misspelled, by mistake or by cunning, the hopeful message of immortality. In practically all these occurrences Death is acknowledged as an unwanted and uncalled for interruption in the flow of life, coming as an undue but inexorable end to all human enterprises.

In India, however, where among the excesses of Tropics, as previously seen, Death is experienced practically at the peak of every season, concern for it assumes a different outlook. Here the end and beginning of everyone and everything is so common that it does not seem that man was ever regarded as potentially immortal "at the beginning", but not even, as a matter of fact, as totally 'mortal' without any hope of a kind of survival in a manner or another. Perhaps, though it is not completely sure, in the more ancient Rigvedic hymns it can be inferred that man shared that privilege with his surely immortal Gods (as they certainly were, like their 'equivalent' Pantheons in the classical national religions of group 2 of the classification presented in the Preface), since Yama is referred to as the First Dead preliminary to his status of King of the inhabitants of the 'Nether-world' toward which he had open the way. The same as the Egyptian Osirides. But, even in this event, one may rather get the impression that Yama did not introduce an end to existence, but on the contrary lead humanity to find a way out toward a more 'solid' and satisfactory after-life. Anyway, in what survives of the Vedic hymns there is not much speculation of what eventually "there was before", the main concern and interest being definitely pointed toward the pragmatical issue of overcoming the damaging effects of Death always there since the beginning and of how to conquer immortality altogether.

Since most ancient time, then, Death was not conceived either as a lost opportunity or as a hopeless coming to an inexorable end. It was, rather, a challenge man had to face by the mere fact of being born into this world, a challenge that had to be met with and fought back through that powerful mean religion put into his hands: rites. In the early Vedic culture funerary rites appear to be inclined toward cremation, but not as a way of destruction of the 'mortal remains' in order to "free the soul" as conceived today, but rather as a manner to "cook"[20] them into perfection in order to transform them into an immortal body ready to be transferred to Heaven (svarga) in the company of the Gods, together with the by-victim burnt with it and sent ahead as a kind of forerunner or announcer of his coming. Such funerary rites are, moreover, conceived as the culmination of a series of domestic as well as solemn rites through which all along his life any caste Indian was supposed (and to some extent is still supposed), at least theoretically, to ransom himself and his wife from the debt to the Gods and eventually to Yama. The fact that, to all practical purposes, it seems that such type of immortality was open to only a small portion of the entire population was not a matter of open social concern, as it could be today under the influence of a different way to tackle collective problems. In the first instance, when those rites were devised the Vedic folk were more compact and homogeneous in their nomadic life than it became later on; then, when sedentary life became the usual mode of existence, together with the related differentiation in castes and works, those listed in the categories excluded from proper Sanskritised rites had their own ways of worship and their own various methods of reaching their destiny's completion, so that Brahmanism was not supposed to be called upon to look after them as well.

Anyway, this totally absorbing endeavour toward conquering immortality became such an important task and goal to be reached that what normally should be seen as an end to be overcome, was turned out to represent the 'starting point' out of which life sprung up into being, in a double stage, first as 'something' stirring out from a cosmic, all-encompassing, original Inertia[21] through the heating process of cooking and offering in a Yajna, and then consolidating itself, through the same sacrificial mean, into a permanent immortality[22]. And so strong was the draw of such initial Inertia and so powerful its hold over everything so that life had to struggle to come into existence, that Brahmanic speculation went so far as to extend Death's grip even to the Gods, the immortals par excellence all over the world, including the main Creator, Prajapati, the Father of the Devas, of the Asuras and of all creatures.[23] If, in fact, life was but a conquest brought about by a perfect performance of appropriate rites and consolidated into immortality by other more specialized forms of cult, there was no reason why such procedure could not apply to every Being, whatever its position in the gerarchical religious setting. The difference between the various categories, then, became only a matter of perfection attained by their respective rites: the Devas were totally successful in their own and became immortal, the Asuras (or Demons) lost their chance through some mistake or other, while men, though somehow also well versed in their sacred efforts, were not totally effective in their results in so far as Death itself complained of being bereft of its due, so that humans had to be contented with a post-mortem immortality after leaving the gross body to its Claimer—an obvious way of acknowledging a hard matter of fact.[24] But, all the same, the very fact of being put on the same footing as the Immortals by right gives Brahmanic man a very good standard with respect of human main desire of survival. If Death is at the beginning for everybody, life is but a process of strengthening one's possibilities virtually to infinity. In this process the Gods got the best lot by assuring to themselves a more or less stable immortality;[25] nevertheless, the fact that even Gods' fate depended by a sacred performance gave men the undying hope that they too one day may struck the right ritualistic perfection and reach a full immortality without having to pay with the loss of the gross-body.[26]

Yet, time and the conquests of meditation are always on the move and before too long, possibly prompted either by increasingly scantier actual opportunities for solemn ritual performances—a fact which forced its technicians to think about them more in theoretical than in practical terms— or by forceful shifts to meditation induced in the sages by their entering in the third and fourth stage of renunciation, or probably by both, religion itself got a turn toward a more spiritualised vision in such a way that even Death became to be conceived in a new way. When, under the deepening effect of interiorization of rites, the very Godhead lost its personality to reveal the unfathomable abysm of Its Absoluteness, then the sages were irresistibly attracted to It so that Death was rather sought after as a way to 'realize' one's sameness with that very Absolute. Thus, the Death placed at the beginning became also the goal to be attained in a quiet dissolution into an overpowering final Death or Divine Essence. The whole process of reaching it by way of detachment and gradually annihilating one's own Karmatic residues become known as Moksa, or Desire for Mukti, that is Liberation. Liberation from the endless chain of lives and deaths brought about by one's own Actions according to the Law of Karman. And when Brahmanism began to be slowly replaced by a more mythical Pauranic set of believes and ritual practices, as we shall going to see soon, such Law provided, at its turn, a new opening toward overcoming the natural horror for Death. If man is but the solidified block of unconsumed effects of his actions, then Death is automatically over-passed in the sense that those "blocks" had to find other means to be resolved when it appears obvious that a person's expiring could not be the end of his accumulated concatenations of actions and counteractions. New lives with new bodies but the same 'karmatic' personality had to come into existence in order to allow that active play to continue till complete resolution into the Mukti of the sages.

The doctrine of Karman, with its development into belief of 'reincarnation', has then provided a new type of neutralization of the terror of Death by taming it into a mere sequence of body's changes into a continuously revolving world of senses or Samsara. Earth itself 'metamorphosises' from a definitive end for most of the people and a passage to immortalization for the few entitled to ransom themselves with adequate rites, into a mere change of forms in an ever-ending chain of subsequent opportunities till the desire of Liberation from all this would push a few ones to cut through it by forcing detachment through ascetic and spiritual exercises.

f. The Law of Karma:

Personal responsibility in social order and in individual growth.

What we have so far described as a cultural structure superimposed to a multivalent world in the attempt to provide it with a unifying interpretation, did not suggest itself immediately to people's awareness, perhaps not even to that of its proposers, as a mould suddenly befalling over an amorphous Reality for the purpose of shaping it to their taste. On the contrary, not only its actual acceptance in society but its very elaboration must have taken various centuries of gestation and an even longer time for becoming an efficient rule of life. Once operative, however, the rigidity of such a compartmentalized structure should not have taken long to raise some uneasiness and perhaps also a certain amount of perplexity. This happened not so much for the inequality so revealed and endorsed (this inequality is a problem that has its catching mainly in the present day awareness, but was accepted as a matter of fact for quite a long time), but especially for the numerous halfway cases of difficult collocation and for those certainly not too rare occurrences of personal aptitudes and inclinations not always attuned with the qualities befitting one's caste by birth. Even in Epics and in ancient historical accounts we come across kings with strong disposition for contemplative mood more appropriate for the priestly layer of population and young Brahmins bent toward acquisition of power and wealth or some ambitious youth aiming at being accepted in princely company. Such occurrences, especially when arising within the leading members of the society responsible for this very situation, must have lead to the problem of which destiny lays behind the attribution of a position rather than another, especially when, in the course of time, the whole system crystallized or froze up into a framework where the only possible entrance in a given caste was through birth. On the same stroke, it also became the necessity of finding out what to do in order to avoid as far as possible such box-like order. Today the same questions and the same problems strain human consciousness in a different manner, by stressing its apparent lack of justice and undue inequality. In both cases, it is basically question of the same fundamental difficulty: how to explain the differences (which, social equalitarianism apart, are unquestionably present in characters, inclinations and aptitudes) and above all how to find a way to leave open possibilities of growth and changes toward improvement.

The sages through personal experience and observations have, as usual, worked out the answer. They argued that, since changes keep on occurring in physiological growth and decay, in intellectual achievements or degenerations, and even in attaining wisdom (generally attached to the process of getting old irrespectively of social situations), so it is reasonable to consider as well the possibility for improving—or worsening—whatever starting situation one happens to find oneself in. On the other side, however, this theorical movement could not properly be applied to the caste system as such, because this belongs to the ritually and religiously worked out Order aiming at keeping in shape social life and cosmic coordinates. Moreover, though sometimes individuals can find their allotted place uncomfortable because unsuited to their nature and character, in the majority of cases people find in their communities the surety of human solidarity together with the acknowledgment of their proper and irreplaceable position in the social and universal structure—which is also a manner to preserve their inner psychological integrity. If one would try to undermine such a configuration, they possibly would argue, the end result could only be a more or less fast process of disintegration of society as such, in the same way in which a cloth is sure to loosen its shape if the threads forming its warp were to get out of place or to become too pliable, or if the knots of a carpet get suddenly slacken or open. Even on further considerations, social structure, as woven by sacrifices through their theoretical interpretation, has its function to perform so that it cannot be dismissed with a light heart. The fact itself that still it maintains its hold in spite of all the attacks launched against it in modern times, even by the Constitution itself, can be taken as a prove for not being a total rubbish. A possible backing of this interpretation can be found in one of the several etymological explanations proposed for the word "yavana"[27] used to designate the ancient Greek merchants established in the country and extended to identify all 'white' foreigners in general (in the same fashion as in modern Hindi the term "angrezi" is applied to all Westerners): from the root ya- meaning "to mix", a possibly denigratory hint to a 'mixed up' population not caring for a well organized society.

A kind of way out for maintaining the system, yet allowing a sort of flexibility in it, could be that of conceiving it through the simile of a house of many rooms each of which is used for a distinctive kind of activity or handicraft. The rooms are filled to capacity with specialized workers fitting the specific enterprise going on in each of them; however, individually the inhabitants may occasionally be shifted into another one after acquiring a new efficiency (or if degrading in skill) in a kind of promotion or degradation in the assembly-chain which life is. It goes without saying, then, that each person is responsible for himself (or, obviously, for herself) for the degree of skill and perfection that he was able to attain. Only later on, supposedly under the impact of foreign invasions and other cultures' influence, the caste system frozen—as seen—in more un-crossable barriers. Yet, occasional exceptions of shifts are not completely ruled out to this day.

But, if belonging to a given "room" is question of skill (which here stands for birth), then it may also mean that the responsibility of finding oneself in a given caste and social position becomes an individual enterprise, decided by the degree of proficiency reached by any subject. To the obvious objection (especially valid today, but possibly intriguing in ancient times too) that such a 'skillness' is handed down to individuals by way of birth and not of 'merits' (or demerits), the causes had to be brought back to previous causes where such merits or demerits could or would have had the possibility to develop. This solution could also have been inspired by everyday experience, where actions are hardly if ever insignificant, in so far as they generally produce and bring with them effects which, at their own turn, foster other collateral and dependent by-effects with potentialities of development not always be foreseeable and therefore avoidable. It can, then, be somehow assumed that these observations at the level of cultural interpretations about arising social problems were the spur that set in motion the formation of what, with time, became to be known as the Law of Karma. Karma, or Karman in its neutral form, is a Sanskrit noun deriving from the root kar, meaning, "to do"; therefore pointing at the Action in which any person is engaged at. In this Law, the activity of everyone is seen as the consolidation in a solid block of effects and counter-effects at first aiming at deciding the success or not of a career, but in proper time ending up by signifying the (trans)formation of such "blocks" into personal entities solidified in Time and Space and located in historical periods, in the bosom of properly appropriated families and castes[28]. At its turn, this vision or world-view soon felt the need to extend its field beyond the stretch of a single life, because experience clearly began to show acts that did not have time and means to carry on, for good or bad, all their potentialities, so that it became rather "obvious" that such actions required longer periods than a single human life for exhausting all their pending effects. This could, then, be taken to accept that the destiny of being born in a situation rather than in another could be due to previously unresolved "blocks of Karma". The measure of time in Yugas raised no problem with respect to the possibility of stretching the length of Karma's operations beyond a single person's short life-span, while the cyclical endless coming back of new circumstances favourable to new flourishing of vitality after seasonal devastations concretely exemplified the possibility of re-births...to infinity if necessary.

Karmic Law, then, acquired on cultural and religious level a prominent position specially because its presence is more and more seen as a kind of suitable explanation of all Brahmanic cultural premises, and then taken up as a unifying element in the multifaced construction of rules and regulations as well as social grouping as presented up to now. The Law of Karma is especially fitted for the individuals, whose growth is harmoniously directed through various physiological and religious stages toward full success or defeat, till gradually moving in the direction of melting away all the effects of Action when, at the entrance in the third stage of life, that of retirement, persons devote their conduct to reach detachment from the fruits and from the adhesions acquired and accumulated during the active period of the second stage; while the full melting and disappearance of the whole "block" would, theoretically, be attained in the fourth stage, that of the renouncer, a stage that can be fully reached even after thousands of years altogether. Due to the fact that often the very thickness of past actions does not allow a full clear up of further potentialities, only few people are allured to enter the cleansing third stage—let alone the difficult fourth one. For the majority of human beings the very heaviness of their Actions would propose itself up again and again in following existences till only a thin residue remains, which could somewhat easily be overcome by the sage who at last reaches this status of detachment. In the same time, the Law of Karma, on the collective social level, becomes the warrant for the legitimacy of different stages of efficiency, preparation, positions (intellectual and in career) according to the various aptitudes and works, and therefore also in the different degrees of religious and spiritual preparation without much frictions with members of other levels. The slow flowing of Time in Yugas supports with patience the slow toil of perfecting oneself through caste ascent, family improvement and personal attainments.

It goes without saying that, in the kaleidoscopic world of the Tropics settled in a vast area, any rigidity can remain valid only to a certain extent. Thus, while emigration in different states and from villages to cities expedites and somehow authorizes admission in different social contexts or while political moves (in modern times) become effective in promoting a social climb in every type of career, so also on religious level, where difference among castes is more evident because essentially based on the ritual principle of Pure and Impure categories, the jump into the last stage, that of the renouncer aiming at perfection beyond any conditioning situation, is available to all, from whatever position a person happen to be. Wisdom is difficult to attain and theoretically the representatives of traditional culture do not conceal their preference for a regular ascent through all classes and castes so that the more natural 'spring-board' into Liberation would be the condition of an orthodox Brahmin; practically, however, realized persons who succeeded in erasing every Karmic residue or to sharply cut any attachment to the fruit of existence come from every status in life...and all of them are equally object of admiration, veneration, wonder...and sought upon as masters and spiritual gurus.

It has to be added here, but only in a hint, that together with the solidity of actions, differentiation in human groups is further specified by the variable exchange in individuals (and their related groups) of three basic "qualities", Gunas represented by satva or purity, goodness, rajas or strength, power, and tamas darkness, heaviness. The variation in human characters and in the elements is essentially due to the proportion in which these three qualities are intermixing with one another. Such a composition, though subjected to—or possibly because subjected to—a consequential rigid chain of causes and effects, is also susceptible of extreme mobility since it is enough to modify the tendency and tenor of one's actions (and feelings) to adequately modify at the same time the proportion of Gunas involved in the individual's formation[29]. However, an elaboration on this doctrine which is essentially philosophical, will lead us too far away from the purposes of this monograph which does not want to be anything more than a survey.

NOTES

1. On Ashramas see again the often quoted P.V.Kane, *History of Dharma Shastra*, chapters VIII, XXVII, XXVIII; P.H.Prabhu, *Hindu Social Organization*, op.cit., ch ; R.K.Mukherjee *Ancient Indian Education (Brahmanical and Buddhist)*, Delhi (Motilal), 1947, especially for the 1st Ashrama.

2. Strabo, *Geography* XV. 1,59, who also adds (ib), always referring to the authority of Megesthenes, that a Brahman in his dwelling in the woods may marry many wives in order to as to beget many children so as to have many helpers and Megesthenes adds that slaves were out of question in India.

3. This specification about the study of the "significance" of the sacred scriptures does not contradict the above mentioned learning of the Vedas by the youth of the 1st Ashrama: the learning of the texts in this 1st stage involves memorization of sounds, without dealing on meaning.

4. This stages is mostly represented by the last portion of the Vedic Texts, the Upanishads

5. The works dealing with this subject are necessarily the same as in the previous group since both belong to the same concern for the individual

6. For detailed references see P.V. Kane, op. cit, Vol II. Ch. 6,7 Rajboli Pandey, *Hindu Sanskaras; Socio Religious Study of the Hindu Sacraments*, 2d Ed. Delhi (Motilal) 1969; H. N. Chatterjee, *Studies in Some Aspects of Hindu Samskaras in Ancient India*, Calcutta (I. PB) 1965; just to quote a few examples.

7. See, e.g, J. Gonda, *"Upanayana"* in *Indologica Taurineusia* 7, Torino (1979) pp 253-59; Brian K.Smith, "Ritual, knowledge, and Being: initiation and Veda study in Ancient India", In Numen, 33, Leyden (1986) pp. 65-89 where the dates of the ritual are anticipated for the ancient times.

8. Cfr references in Note (6) most of what described about this "sacrament"— besides the written reference—is derived also from personal direct witnesses.

9. See the general references quoted above (Note 6).

10. See the general references of Note (6), to which could be added the research of J.Vigne, *Le Maitre at le Therapeute. Un psychiatrist en Inde*, Paris (A. Michel)

1993 {English transl, by U.M.Vesci, *The Indian Teaching Tradition (A Psychological and Spiritual Study)*, Delhi (B.R. Publ.Corp.) Delhi 1997}

11. See the general references quoted above (Note 6).

12. See Ram Gopal, *India of the Vedic Kalpasutra*, Delhi (N.P.H) 1959.

13. See also Brian K. Smith, *Reflection on Resemblance, Ritual, and Religion*, Delhi (Motilal) 1998 (orig. 1989) p.92 ff.

14. See RV.X.34.10 where a gambler is said to be totally indebted (ṛṇāvā).

15. For the doctrine of debt or of duty due to the different categories described below see Manu, III 68-70 & 73-74, See also Ch. Malamoud, *"La Theologies de la dette dans le brahmanism"* in *Purusārtha 4* (1980). pp 39-62.

16. On this respect see the comment of Brian K.Smith, op.cit. p.20. ff who points cut that , though the whole Brahmanism and Hindusim are based and built up on the Vedas and the Vedic Authority, in practice the Vedas are unknown to the majority of Indians. Cf also one book review by an Indian scholar to my previous book on *Vedic Sacrifice* (op. cit) who found strange that all foreigners (like Max Mullers, etc.) dealing with Vedic Subjects are involved with subject matters, quite obsolete and of *no interest* for the Indians.(quote).

17. See, for instance, the sin of Adam in the Bible of the Hebrew the cunning of Prometheus, in Greek Mythology (Hes.) who, in his eagerness to help Men having the more eatable portion in the sacrifice, bestows also death on them; the different Mythologies of the Ethic People (Frazer); the Babylonian tale of Gilgamesh and so on.

18. In the Brahmanas (see later) Death is so powerful that threaten even Prajapati on and again Sat Br VI.1.2.12; VII. 7.4.2.1ff; X.1.1.1.etc.)

19. See RV. I. 35.6 where the "abode of Yama" is said to be the highest; or RV X.14.1-2 where the same Yama is said to have found the way for men; etc.

20. See the concerned chapter on Death on my quoted book, *Heat and Sacrifice in the Vedas*, ch II.1.c. (p.40f). For Vedic Texts see RV.X.14 to 16.

21. Though in the hymn of Creation (RV.X.129.2) it is stated that, prior to any surging of Beings not even Death (Mrityu) was there; but neither was immortality (Amirtam) present

22. This, actually, is the main concern of many rituals (see later).

23. See Sat Br X.4.3.9

24. See Sat Br XI.2.3.6' etc; TaittSam. II. 3.2.1; PancBr XXIV. 19.2 etc.

25. It is said "more or less" because in further development through meditation even the status of Deva is bound to come to a kind of termination and only the position of man can become the starting point for a jump into total freedom, as is would be seen later

26. As the Yajmana of old over against the larger lot of common people (in Vedic times).

27. See M. Monier Williams, *Sanskrit English Dictionary*, (sub voce Yavana 2) (p. 848). The connection with Yavana 1 is done by me.

28. See P.V. Kane, op. cit, Vol V pt. 2, cht. 35 and for an exhaustive presentation W.Doniger O' Flaherty (ed.) *Karma and Rebirth in Classical Indian Tradition*, (Univ. of Calif.), 1980 reprint Delhi (Motilal), 1983.

29. See e.g. M.Hiriyamna, *Outlines of Indian Philosophy*, London, (G.H. Univia), 1964, pp 271 ff: and S.Chatterjee & D.Datta, *An Introduction to Indian Philosophy*, Calcutta (Univ. of Calcutta) 1968, pp.257 ff.

PART III

RELIGIOUS COORDINATES:

INTRODUCTION
Religion of Wisdom and Popular Religion

It should be rather clear by now that whatever has been presented up to this point cannot be considered a vision built up merely on social and political premises, but sinks its roots deeply down a complex religious conception. The fact that here, and yet simply on ground of expediency, the two portions, the 'worldly' social one and the "out-worldly" or religious, are dealt with in separate chapters does not mean that such division ever existed in the awareness of those who have laboured to establish this whole cultural compartmentalized foundation. As a matter of fact, except for 'modern' mentality, a similar separation between a lay settlement and a religious level concerned only with disembodied souls and their after-life salvation, never existed in any culture, included Western Christianity till after Renaissance[1]. Man has been always seen as a whole made up of body and soul and both had to be cared for together and judiciously guided to their respective fulfilment whatever it would be. In India this wholeness is even more evident than elsewhere. Its world-vision (Weltanschauung), in fact, sprung up and took an external, social and political form as the practical projection of its religious experience concretised through well-elaborated rites. This means that the real and deep significance of what has been presented so far can be understood only when its reason is sought after in the religious Order (dharma), which gave it its theoretical basis. As already hinted at, this 'Order' is, on the one hand, the product and, on the other, the leading motive of the Vedic Sacred Action called Yajna, which it is now time to be properly introduced.

CHAPTER I
Religion of Vedic Wisdom

It has been already seen that the people responsible for the construc tion and spreading of the main culture which has given the country its present feature was a group of well organized tribes originally living in the mountain areas of North-West India (actual Afghan and North Pakistan/ Panjab) and then swooping down on the Gangetic plains possibly in search of new and better pastures for their main wealth and possession: cattle. Such people, like those related tribes that had chosen West and North-West for their displacement, worshipped a rather well characterized Pantheon of Divine figures bearing, by and large, a rather close affinity among those of the various groups. This affinity struck European scholars who, around the middle of XIXth century, came in contact again with India and began to know India's ancient religious texts. Such affinities lead them to hypothesize the theory of a common origin from a reconstructed Indo-European race or even nation. Though not always bearing the same names, it is quite beyond doubt that the early Vedic Gods as praised in the hymns, especially of Rigveda and Atharvaveda, are the counterpart of many of the main Deities of Roman, Greek and German Pantheons, often sharing the same basic characteristics. All recall a further away early couple of a Sky Father and a Mother-Earth, faded into a faint past memory in order to allow a 'younger generation' to take over as rulers of the Universe and of earthly human beings. These 'new' Gods include, among others, especially a 'sovereign' with warrior-like attributes and a mastering over the thunderbolt (Indra, equivalent of Zeus, Juppiter and Wotan), a twin couple of young healers (the Asvins, equivalent to the Greek and Roman Dioscuroi), many Goddesses out of whose a triade takes the upper hand, and a Deity connected with Fire. Though Roman and Greek depository and protector of such element, but not the element itself, is a Goddess (Vesta and Hestia respectively), the Vedic equivalent is a God: Agni (the same word used in Latin to mean fire, the element, ignis) who is that very element and is deeply and intensely connected with the already mentioned type of Sacrifice called Yajna. A comparative study about Yajna and similar rites as found in ancient Greece and Roma reveals a wealth of similarities and few significant differences that could, if properly pursued, disclose new features, meanings and purposes in all the three religions concerned, together, perhaps, with the causes of at least some among the differences in their respective doctrines, philosophies and mythologies.[2]

However, notwithstanding the abundance of details offered by the above-mentioned Vedic Hymns, it is not always easy to reach a properly exhaustive reconstruction of the actual form assumed by the performance of Yajna in those very ancient times. It is possible that the Yajna transpiring from Hymns'references were simpler than those described and elaborated by their exegetical literature: the Brahmanas and the Sutras. And this not because, as often presumed with respect to an 'early' mentality, the practitioners of early Vedic rites had not 'reached' a more complex form of reasoning (often a mentality working on premises valid in ancient times is much more complicated than more recent developments almost as human 'growth' would be more a process of simplification than of accumulation), but rather because the living conditions of the people performing them, coupled smoothly with their usual surroundings, were somehow more homogeneous and therefore more easy to cope with. They could somehow be managed with relatively simple rites going straightaway to the point in hand. In the existential frame in which these warriors' groups were moving and to which they were accustomed, both landscape and weather were known and manageable entities that possibly needed only keeping on going through those rites envisaged for any purpose more or less in the same manner as among most people of the world—each according to their local environment—so that their respective 'specialists of the Sacred' had more leisure to concentrate on what was keener to their immediate needs: to ensure increasing of valuable warriors through successfully begetting strong sons, to secure victory over enemies and protection against the latter's magic devices, and also to consolidate their riches by protecting their cattle and by increasing them through raids against members and cattle of other tribes of the same folk. In other words, their World-vision was rather uniform and the rites operating in it were adapted to its rhythms. The main bulk of population was also relatively compact and all the members actively intermixed on the same related tasks: fighting and raising cattle on the practical level, supported and guided religiously by the priests on doctrinal and ritualistic levels.[3]

Things became different when, in the momentous event of crossing the boundaries of the 'known land' of their abitual territories many such tribes came down on the Indian plains and were faced with the geographical and climatic conditions we have previously outlined. This problem, however, could be described not so much as the question of dealing with people of different racial features, different costumes and different (therefore incomprehensible and enigmatic) ways of life. All over human history round the globe, meeting with totally different races and behaviours does not create real serious problems; the totally different cannot even be perceived let alone understood, so the usual way is to get rid of it by sweeping away the people embodying it when it could be done, or enslave them when mass destruction reveals itself to be impossible. Or, if the impact would be resolved negatively, by absorbing them into one's own mythology as representing a temporary victory of darkness—which in the case of Indians such was not to be the case for centuries to come. The real problem was posed to the priests and exegetes by the changes in their habitat, now too wide, too full, too uncertain; and also by the new drive in living that such habitat imposed to all groups: sedentary settlements. Plains did not offer endless pastures, but, as compensation, provided the opportunity for producing food through agricultural cultivation. As known all over through the same process occurring to the majority of nations when setting down to a new way of living in fixed surroundings, also the Vedic people had to cope with that big change in their way of life, which naturally had to call for a new way of looking at nature and of interpreting it in the light of a new cultural relationship. Moreover, sedentary life required rather soon a specialization of duties, widening in this way the gap— before hardly perceivable—between the members of the same tribes, and adding to the lot a quickly increasing population of local folks drawn into their cultural orbit together with children born of mixed marriages or through concubines; while, in the same trend, specialization brought about also a differentiation in incomes and 'political' influences. All this, presenting itself with the strength and virulence of the Tropics, struck the people, responsible for the cultural and religious (under)-standing of their nations, with the urgent need of being coped with in a new and different way from the usual one. They perceived that all those differences risked to plung them all over again into cultural chaos and, in order to avert the danger to be drowned in it or, worst of all (for them) to see their tribes to settle in separate units (liable to forget their common background), they had to create a new system of coordinates that could keep Reality harmoniously organized once more in a comprehensible Whole—though maintaining as far as possible their individual peculiarities—and reinterpreted in a way that could again make sense for the whole 'nation'.[4]

This effort is still amply detectable in what remains of the ancient sacred literature: especially the Yajurveda with its Brahmanas and Sutras, but also the other Brahmanas together with, possibly, a new arrangement of their ancient Rigvedic, Sama and Atharvavedic hymns. This literature, which we are going to sketch out further down, is a very complex one and is mainly concerned with ritual practices. It is, virtually, our only source about Vedic solemn sacrifices and guides us to their intricacies both in a down to the letter way of performing them and in a more interpretative mood through philosophical as well as mythological considerations. Due to what has been said about the impossibility to keep linear record of a sequential past in this country, we have to rely on external data for a probable time when Vedic people began to raise in political and cultural power in the "Land of the Five Rivers" (Panjab)—a time which has been established around 2000 BC, more or less at the same date in which cognate tribes entered Middle Asia and Europe—while the settling down with the elaboration of Brahmanas and Sutras is placed around the IX-VIIIth century BC, also in accordance with the contemporary arising of Greek and Etruscan/Roman civilizations. From inner data, what can be fairly inferred is that the content of the Rigvedic and Atharvavedic hymns go back several centuries in a past mostly lost to memory. But this past for some reasons or other, possibly under the impact of that change of life just mentioned, became important again in order to provide solid roots to fall upon as background to new conditions, and as a way to strengthening the thin cultural bond among their tribal kingdoms.

So it was on the strength and basis of such a common past that the competent specialized persons were forced to reconsider their main ritualistic points and adapt them to the new task of dealing with a reality (cultural and geographical at the same time) difficult to handle. The traditional Yajna, in all its various forms and types, had to be thought over again and its aims stretched to cover different situations and to explain (that is, to give a comprehensible interpretation to) a new reality emerging in their awareness as based on premises different from those their people were accustomed to in their previous nomadic life fostering a nomadic culture, which became the model of a 'lost paradise' that had to be remembered at all costs. To complicate things even further, the new setting mostly discouraged their ex chieftains to get involved for long stretch of time into active performance of enlarged and expensive Yajnas, now appearing less essential for assuring immediate victory over the enemy;

while, at the same time, such performances were vitally needed for the priestly class in order for them to work out the new purposes and new cultural coordinates of a different life in a different surrounding. Brahmanas and Epics show us that, during those rather few occasions of actual performances of solemn Yajnas, the priestly class, assisted by the authority of some important sages and philosophers, were strenuously busy in explaining, planning, re-setting and reinterpreting the main features of their predominant sacred actions. They, undoubtedly, revitalized those hymns still preserved in their memory, re-enacted gestures and procedures that seem to have become obsolete—since they had to be recollected and settled again in verses and prose in order to show again how they should be performed and in what sequence and for what reasons. Many a time the Brahmanas seem engaged in recovering the meaning of lost myths, hinted upon in the hymns, either by reconstructing them through the small fragments still available or by inventing them again altogether.[5] It was in these circumstances that, in order to cover every possible features, Yajna became a huge Festival session, with ever increasing rituals and a more and more complicated structure, leaving ample time, in the hours between actual cultic performances, for theoretical discussions and specialized instructions to the high caste people; the gist of these discussions and teachings were collected in a vast literature: the very Brahmanas. Their task of gathering, adapting, reinterpreting and explaining all the ritualistic possibilities, ended up by creating new cosmologies and cosmogonies, together with a new conception altogether of the Divine as such. And this is when Brahmanism as such was founded or built up, standing for an everlasting Present on which a far distant Past was incorporated and a possible Future contained in its in-built potentialities towards exoteric expressions and developments. In this way, it can be noticed that the people "who could not have a historical feeling" could manage to supply on their own manner a marking of time which could suit them well at every moment of their individual and cultural life.

The most important task, in this literature, has been that of founding, practically all over again, a new World-view and a new cosmology, with its related cosmogonies, together with a new cultural and social vision. Reality in front of them posed new problems different from those they were accustomed to deal with in the mountains. The Yajurveda, with its various schools (an indication that thinking activities went on simultaneously in many places) and its Brahmanas, suggest this type of brooding and bubbling with ideas that had to fit into a more suitable cultural and religious presentation, though without rejecting their roots still sinking deep into a past that once was familiar to them. The Sutras fixing ritual rules and the Brahmanas of the other traditional and more ancient clusters of hymns (the Rigvedic and Atharvavedic, together with the Samavedic rearrangement in suitable liturgical chants) were added to this huge material in this impressive elaboration of texts, rites, cosmology, all melted together to form a new coherent cultural and religious construction, into the birth of the real Indian culture. The traditional feeling that, whatever the Indological scholars may say regarding the historically ancient content of the Rigveda and Atharvaveda, their hymns are later arrangement fixed by the Brahmanas and Sutras—which have to be placed earlier, thus not totally fitting with the respective cultures reflected in them—is thus correct and meaningful if one accepts the fact that the Brahmanas and the Sutras are the central pillars and the starting point of the full Brahmanic construction[6], which reach to their pre-history in a way homologable (but not on the same spirit) to that of the Greeks looking back at the Homer's heroes as their ancestors, or of the Romans regarding Eneas of Troy as their progenitor.

All this must have taken some centuries of gestation and elaboration brought about in relative isolation by the royal family priests (purohitas) regularly engaged in their domestic ritual procedures, and occasionally confronted with parallel toiling of other collegues in the rare occurrences of some important Yajnas. These events, being by now even more a rarity than before, were obviously more valued by the 'experts', who took gladly the opportunity for meeting together and discussing points of particular bearing and significance. Epics and Brahmanas offer some hints about such meaningful events. This creative effervescence must have lasted again for several centuries when layer over layer of additions, droppings and reshapings must have been going on without leaving any trace of a possible linear sequence, till everything must have been definitely settled during a huge gathering (or possibly two closely correlated ones in two forest's locations near to one another at Kurukshetra and Naimisaranya)[7]. Here, possibly around the VI-Vth century BC—if we can trust the tendency in human history of having thing culturally and religiously happening in contemporary waves of time—[8] the whole Vedic Corpus was rearranged, fixed and divided in its canonical parts, thus bringing it to its close. This means that by that time tradition had reached its completeness and, from then on, got frozen into a block, sinking again, at its own turn, into the past. From now on philosophers, exegetes, grammarians, ritualistic experts could only exercise their skill through comments and interpretations without the possibility of adding anything to the bulk of that Sacred Knowledge.

Their task extended also to the preservation of such Knowledge through recitation and commitment to memory. In fact, though still used in some cases during actual performances, by now even more rare than before, the transmission of such a cultural and religious wealth was shifted, perhaps right from the time of those important and meaningful gatherings just mentioned above, into reiterated recitations and the transforming power previously developed in the Sacred Actions was transferred to the equivalent power aroused in and released through the sound of the ritually recited Words. This change, as we shall see later, was not without consequences and, in time, gave rise to a 'new' religious setting altogether (of course, as far as any 'newness' can ever be possible in such a conservative country as India is).

a. Rites: solemn and domestic

i) Yajna, Shrauta rites.

As stated above, one of the specific and most important rites of Vedic period is Yajna, a designation derived from the Sanskrit root *yaj*-to worship. It could be better translated with the English term "ceremony", "festivities" held for special occasions, but I prefer to retain the most usual term: "Sacrifice", provided that it is not taken in its current (modern) meaning of "renunciation" (in Sanskrit: *tyag*), but is understood in its Latin etymology. Sacrifice comes, in fact, from the Roman *sacri-ficium* and is a compound of sacrum, meaning "sacred", and *facere*, meaning to "do", thus approaching its Sanskrit equivalent: Karman, Action. Sacrifice can, therefore, be translated as "performance of a (sacred) Action" or with the expression: "doing something sacred". Such Action, carried on in a solemn way, is a complex one involving several connected rites and spanning through long periods, varying in length from one or few days to some months, from the standard measure of one year to several of them up to twelve's or more. Actually, though partaking of sacrificial remnants is confined specifically to the Yajamana, his wife and his offering priests, the event is so important that it usually gathers on the spot most of the more prominent friends and subjects of the performer together with plenty from neighbouring kingdoms. All of them enjoy special entertainments and a good choice of food, though not from the selected sacred offerings. As far, instead, as offerings are concerned, generally they consist of a main item (like Soma, for instance, or a Horse, or Milk and milk products, or other ingredients (including the sacrificer's own body on the funeral pyre at his death)) surrounded by other accompanying by-offerings, ranging from grain or rice-cakes or puddings to animal immolations in which case the he-goat is the most common item. These offerings are carried on at the 'canonical' times of evenings and mornings, and sometimes also at mid-day and their main features are to be cooked (often on a fire-place specially built for this purpose, the Garhapatya) and then poured on the main Fire in the 'offertory' Fire-altar (Ahavaniya). Fire, Agni, as already hinted upon, is a God and a very important one in the Vedic Pantheon. In the religious view of the ancient Hymns, especially the Rigvedics as reinforced and reinterpreted in the Brahmanas, He is the Mediator between men and Gods, because it is He who transforms the man-made offerings into divine items through cooking, and it is He who receives in himself the final product and delivers it to its heavenly destination.

There are many types of Yajna and some traditions (as that of the Atharvans, for instance, reported by their Brahmana, the Gopatha) have divided them into three sets of seven[9]. Others, instead, dwell upon a division where five gets the upper hand[10]. Of the more convenient partition of twenty-one Yajnas, the first set refers to seven different kinds of Soma Pressings, the second concerns an equal number of sacrifices characterised by their "cooked offerings" and thus called "pakayajna", while the third, called "haviryajna", deals with more common types of offerings. We do not need to enter into more detailed descriptions here, since there is already a vast ancient and modern literature taking care of this, and I have already touched upon the subject in a previous work.[11] Here the main issue being that of outlining the cultural spirit underneath the whole ritualistic construction, it is sufficient to have simply sketched the Vedic conception of sacrifice, which accounts as much for the social and political structure of the whole culture and civilization as for its religious attainments and organization, together with an open perspective for a free development of individuals according to their personality and inner achievements. It also accounts for the place of honour accorded, at least theoretically, to the priestly class, and their caste as a whole.

Yajna, however, is not a compulsory ceremony, which has to be regularly performed according to cyclical recurrences, like festivals, for instance, that, as we have seen, mark changes of seasons or celebrate some fixed astronomical cyclical events. If offered at all, it normally requires a definite purpose on an individual level and the all roundabout is set in motion just to fulfil that purpose. It comes to a definitive end when such objective has been reached. And generally, except when the acquisition of an immortal body is at stake, such purposes not only concern the welfare and objectives of important individual persons, but are also deeply rooted in this very world and have concrete mundane aims. Almost as 'by-products'—or this is at least the impression that often can be gathered from the pertinent texts—Order is settled in the Universe, full cosmogonies find their achievements, cultural patterns are worked out and applied to the living practical reality, while all along the priests' main concern deals with the welfare of his single 'sponsor', the sacrificer or Yajamana, and the attainment of his occasional desire (be it a son, more wealth in form of riches or villages over which to rule, or the attainment of an immortal body with which to get transferred in Heaven (svarga) after death). So, at its turn, this situation introduces another anomaly in the smooth understanding of Brahmanic culture: in the country dominated by a sense of an eternally cyclic time, measured in spans of Yugas, the 'sacrificial time' is linear, exhibiting a beginning and concluding with an explicitly unappellable end. The very place in which that sacrifice was performed (a special area separated from the sacrificer's home, built for the occasion according to specific rules and requirements) is totally destroyed after the allotted period is over and all actions completed; and where, in the special occurrence of the erection of a baked bricks altar, this destruction becomes impossible, the construction itself with its surroundings is desecrated and interdiction imposed to the whole area. This external location of the altar, together with its totally removal and destruction at the end of the performance's period spell clearly of the will to maintain intact for ever the memory and the feeling of the original nomadic past of the warriors following their moving cattle into new pastures. Since, however, especially if the ceremony under performance (or under study) is one lasting over several years, the main offerings are repeated at regular intervals (either daily evenings and mornings, or monthly on lunar phases, or seasonally) as long as its previously fixed period comes to its unavoidable conclusion, many a scholar, prompted by the homologable examples in other stately religions and by some internal references in Vedic texts of cyclical (theoretical) recurrences, have come up with the idea that, "at least in the past", such solemn events were going on indefinitely on regular bases, engaging rulers and their priestly cohorts all along their active career, even on the scale of being compulsory for all the adult members of the privileged castes[12]. A deeper reading into the texts and a confrontation with local practices and priestly authority show, however, that this was not the case even in the Brahmanic times, and that is why any happening of this kind along history has been always considered much high and has held such a degree of interest as to amounting to real fascination[13]. That is also the reason why such a detailed literature was developed on rites in general and on each event in particular: things had to be recorded (either by memory or by written stuff) in order to be available when an opportunity of this kind would be raised...sometimes even after centuries. In this respect, Brahmanic literature stands at a pair with the Hebrew sacred Scriptures, which were first collected in a given pattern during Babilonian exile and then further elaborated during the definitive Diaspora after the destruction of the Temple of Jerusalem. This means that most of those rules thus recorded were recollected, meditated and interpreted in various fashions only in periods in which performances were impossible and the compilers of those highly technical and liturgical treatises never witnessed personally what they were describing. For the Vedic priests and sages such a possibility was not totally ruled out, but it was so rare that practically the whole affair amounted more to a theoretical intellectual exercise than a pragmatic enterprise. This, practically, confirms to the fact that detailed ritualistic procedures enjoyed the privilege of a huge and specialised Sacred Literature only when practical performances were noticeably lacking, while where sacrificial rites were going on, on a regular basis (like among the Greeks, Romans, Germans, just to quote a few) such exegetical texts were not required therefore are missing.

Such a state of things was, indeed, very propitious for unfolding those religious and spiritual views for which India is now becoming more and more famous. From a profound evaluation of Yajna's outcomes and repercussions the social arrangement and coordinates we have just examined in the previous part did stem out, and, besides, a whole series of parallels between this world and the heavenly ones was elaborated so as to reach the conviction, soon amounting to certainty, of a steady correspondence between the universe at large, with its sense of Void and Immensity, the so called "macrocosm", and the innermost depth of human heart, the "microcosm" of each individual[14]. This outcome was, somehow, facilitated, as we are not tired to repeat, by the rarity of real ritual practices which forced the specialists to find good reasons for publicising the advantages those sacred actions could offer to their possible sponsors, while a mere abstract reasoning and recitations began to be presented as equally powerful means for liberating those transforming inner energies able to act at a spiritual level[15], as we are going to see later.

In a certain sense, then, it is not too far fetched to assume that, though rarely performed, Yajna sacrifice has moulded the entire Brahmanic world, being responsible for the four-fold division—on the basis of 3+1—of its whole cultural reality and also for attaining a fairly good blending between social unity and individual independence, through building up a perfect Dharma in the worldly level of collectivity and through leading the individual beings to Mokhsa, or Liberation. On the whole, in fact, Yajna is considered less an offering to some Deities than a wholesome Action constructed in such a way as to 'weave' the texture of creation and to organize the whole Universe into a proper Order, Rita, in which everything and everyone has its, her, his proper place and role to play. Drawing a parallel with other religions, Yajna takes somehow the place of that Mythical Action which, in a manner or another according to each World-view, started things moving and was the final act responsible of the cultural setting of any given population[16]. The main difference is that, while among the others such an Action is purely 'other-worldly' and took place outside Time in the mythical "before the Beginnings", with more often than not, catastrophic or delunding results for the "historical" set up, Yajna was something with positive results, that could be performed here on earth, as it is still occasionally performed.[17]

Agnichayana: In Yajna, as stated before, there are no Divinities present in their images; however, through the myth regarding Prajapati and his fear of dying after his creation, a murti is introduced also in the balk of the Yajnic non-dualistic mood. In the Brahmanas there is the description of a rite, complete with a myth underlining, in a certain sense, its strangeness and extraneity to the whole Vedic structure, that may be seen and interpreted as an attempt of the Pauranic Puja's[18] mentality to step over, or overlap into, the Vedic world-view, though without producing a proper and permanent breach in it. This rite is the optional building an extra Fire-altar, constructed by piling up five layers of baked bricks—thus rendering it indestructible, that is "immortal" in the text's phraseology. The myth clearly supports this view by openly stating that the piling up and the baking of the clay and water material is, according to one version the "cooked oblation" that the Gods put on the Sacred Fire to "recreate" their Father "dead of having created" the worlds[19] or, according to another is the God-sacrifice himself—since nothing else existed except Agni, his first born—who, during an elaborate reasoning about the better way of recovering his lost splendour together with his waning life, finds out the solution of putting it on Fire through various stages: first he thought to hunt for Agni in order to incorporate his brilliancy again, then, seeing that the latter has taken refuge in the five main 'animals' considered to be the most suitable for sacrificial immolation, He gets hold of them and took up their heads for embedding them in the layers of the altar deemed to represent his body; further on, He collected the clay and water where the corpses of the victims have been thrown and with it formed a square brick, with four corners like the Earth. Finally, however, in the act of lying it down the main God perceived that "in doing so with the raw mixture, he could not get rid of Death. He then backed it into the Fire"(ibidem), because He considered that the only item really "immortal" that Vedic culture has ever produced is the "oblation" that has been passed through fire and poured into it after its transformation through cooking. And the Fire really produced the wonder of converting these two 'mortal' elements—mortal because ready to be separated again any time—into an irreversible, therefore 'immortal', terracotta brick. All the other bricks, already explained as oblations of the Gods, are then submitted to the same treatment and the resulting effect is the coming into being of a solid construction defeating damage by time therefore standing beyond the grasp of Death. Not for nothing the new altar is viewed as "the immortal body of Prajapati", that is to say as his permanent Murti.

This erection, however, created a discordant note in the Brahmanic trend toward a non-dualistic pursue of human growth and divinisation. In the whole myth, with its gradual evolving in subsequent steps, is visible the priestly struggle to resist giving up to the mounting influence of common religiosity with a dualistic bent toward a Divinity projecting Itself outside men into Something 'alien', 'different', no longer growing inside selected Yajamanas, but arising as a tangible Alterity. The image coming from that religious world dominated by Puja was a warning about the 'danger' of 'loosing' God altogether if allowing Him to disperse into his creation and especially in the innermost secret portion of human hearts. The priests had to accept the challenge and build something 'solid' to prevent such 'dissolution'. In this way, a Murti was actually inserted into the Yajnic sequence. Yet, the ancient Purohitas were clever enough not to succumb totally to the new, easier, mood. They retained their main non-dualistic consistency by a few ingenious devises: first of all, the Murti they accepted for their Sacrificial Godhead, Prajapati the Lord of the creatures, was not a statue raising as an alien body for the external worship of devotees, but an Altar, that is a spot where a personal Action was taking place and an action is always something movable difficult to pin down; secondly, since the goal or task of sacrifice was the 'immortalization' of the sacrificer, they linked the double immortalisation by identifying even more openly such sacrifice with the main Godhead through the insertion of an image in gold of the human sponsor in the very centre of the first layer of the Murti-to-be, so producing a strong, unbreakable, bondage between Prajapati, Agni and the sacrificing Man. Furthermore, afraid of the remote possibility that after all a solid personification of a Deity could sooner or later produce the temptation of stepping into a dualistic external cult no longer involving the full inner participation of the sacrificer into his own growth and immortality (a thing that eventually really happened), they, notwithstanding the dualistic drive toward the contrary, kept on stressing the impermanency of the whole affair by: first, shaping the Murti as a flying away Bird with fully spread wings, and, then, by foiling the indestructibility of the piled baked bricks by declaring the whole area 'taboo', unapproachable after its sacrificial role was over with the sacrificial action as such. The given, acceptable, reason was that, like the ephemeral statues of the festivals, also these construction had once been the receptacle of the Divine and, though desacrilised, were still dangerous. But this was mainly a way, through shape and interdiction, to reiterate once more their message stating: "it is not good for men to lean for too long on external help for their spiritual growth". In other words, Vedic religion succeeded in maintaining its hold (later shared by the misunderstood Founder of Christianity) that "it is good for (humans)" that God does not linger around as a supporting grouch for too long a time. Another danger avoided by the interdiction of approaching the altar-murti is the temptation of using again the effort of others without bothering to toiling oneself over the whole sacred action.

ii) Domestic rites (Grhya Sutras)

However, since there is no religion without its proper practice and ritual devices, also Vedic people got their existence and their cultural world rightly framed through the so called "domestic rites", Grhya yajna[20], where the Fire involved was not that special one built up in the sacrificial ground, but the household fire, enkindled for every householder at the moment of his marriage. It is this fire that receives the attentions of the adult male of the house in his daily worships; that receives its due at the hands of the housewife before meals, and especially that plays the leading role in whatever ceremony goes on in the house, such as the sacraments (samskaras), for instance, like marriage, birth of a baby, reaching boyhood of sons (still dependents on the paternal fire), and others on various occasions, such as, for example, the opening of an activity (business, trading, learning...) or the inauguration of a new residence...Most of these rites, besides having household fire as their focus; involve as well recitations from the

Sacred Vedic lore. However, with the steady spreading out of a more popular and more commonly reachable, for the average person, 'mythological' literature during the last many centuries, as we are going to see in the next chapter, also texts from the Epics and the Puranas came to be used for such domestic rituals as already seen.

b. The priests and the texts: Purohitas and Vedas

Coming back to the main supporting Sacrificial Action, it can be seen that, in order to function, Yajna needs standing on two essential pillars: 1) the words accompanying the offerings in tune with the different cultic actions, and 2) the priests accomplishing and reciting them. These two are ever present whenever and wherever a sacrificial Action takes place in whatever religion it may be. Their role may or may not be particularly stressed; words may be reduced to short formulas and priestly duties left in charge either of the king (patron of the country he belongs to), when cults are performed at a common social level, or of the householder, when occurring in the personal premises of one's family. However, both have to be there and when their complexity grew in order to cover all possible problems and requirements of arising situations a specialized class of learned and skilful priests was the outcome in practically all the 'national' Theims all over the world.[21] Brahmanism could hardly be expected to be an exception. On the contrary, all pointed toward an extra-ordinary development of both these features, which were already part and parcel of the distant Past they had to woven again into the texture of a Present in the process of getting established on new sedentary basis. Hymns as accompanying words to the Sacred Action in hand had already a long history at their backs and needed to be rearranged into patterns easy available when their use would be required, together with new compositions to be freshly created to cope with different situations; priests, as the man-power engaged in the difficult task of performing, reciting, adapting and interpreting those very Sacred Actions they were involved with, had also to be 'organized' in order to be able, through specialization, to withstand the difficult and articulated tasks pending on them.

But here, again, the task of the chronicler, wanting to maintain a certain order of exposition, proofs once more difficult to realise. Normally, faced with two sets of subjects to deal with as apparently different from one another as a set of sacred formulas and the priests attending to them and to the Action the latter have to be inserted in, a writer has only to decide over the order of precedence to be accorded to one in preference to the other, and then proceed accordingly. Many books consulted on the matter do exactly this, sharply separating the Sacred Texts from the priests dealing with them[22]. Yet, in a work like the present one, which stresses rather the spirit behind the whole apparatus than engaging in a mere exposition of facts, these two sets, i.e. these two pillars of Yajna: the Word and the Priest, are so strictly bound together that practically they overlap, making the task of separating them almost an impossible enterprise. To all purposes, in fact, the priests and the tradition they represent, were identified practically since their beginnings, each set representing the embodiment of the other[23].

This is due, possibly, to the character of strict 'orality' applied to its composition and transmission, an 'orality' persisting long after other human religious traditions had been committed to writing. Oral transmission, in fact, is by no means restricted to Vedic tradition as such, but belongs, practically, to all human cultures, from the so called 'illiterate' civilizations down to the 'national' ones. The Greek Homeric poems, just to quote a couple of instances among an infinite variety of them, had a long oral tradition behind them before they were committed to writing and, in Athens, submitted to a kind of 'critical edition' (to use a modern term) worked out by a school of professionals sponsored by Pisistratos (VIth cent. BC) as part of his cultural and legal arrangement of the City-state he had come to rule. But, once written down in a kind of 'reliable text', their content became the backbone of the Greek religious culture—together with the works of Esiodos—and was taught in schools as part of the curriculum. Also the Jews wrote down their religious Sacred Texts more or less in the same period (middle of VIth cent. BC or a bit later), thus resting on the assurance that the Word of God and the Tradition of the Fathers was faithfully kept and could be handed down to future generations. According to many evidences, the India of the VIth cent. BC also felt the allure of the Times and got busy systematising its cultural heritage in a fix Corpus—or rather a plurality of Corpuses—possibly during one or perhaps two famous Sacrificial Sessions at Kurukshetra (for the Vedic Lore) and Naimisaranya (for the Epics and more 'popular' sacred literature)—we shall return to the latter in the next chapter. It is not excluded that, at least in Naimisaranya, writing was not banned as a mean for recording. After all, for centuries onwards, copying Epical and Puranic texts has been considered as a pious act and perhaps also a powerful agent to arouse religious power. Possibly, judging from the fact that after all manuscripts of Vedic Mantras exist even if of a later date, a written help for helping memory was not totally ruled out even for the Vedas; but what is sure is that even at that juncture tradition unanimously refused any external technical device for transmitting the

Sacred Words, which had to remain Words, i.e. Sound. Thus, orality was fixed as a rule. However, Vedic orality in the very act of asserting its rights of persistence—saving in this way not only the perpetuation of the Sound together with the content, but also the Secrecy such mantras had to be surrounded with if they had to retain their inner creative and at times also healing powers—brought about a radical transformation in the mood itself of that traditional transmitting means. Oral tradition, whenever is still practised in the world, is somehow an open one and give to its 'specialists' the right and possibility to go on changing, adapting and improving according to the circumstances. The same is still valid today with Puranic presentations and interpretations, and with local storytellers of particular regional or castal traditions.

Regarding the Vedas, instead, the priests or the Brahmins in charge of the matter, found themselves at the crossing point of two tendencies: the necessity of continuing to hand down a tradition orally and the fact that such a tradition was no longer open but has been systematised into a fixed and unchangeable Bulk (which accounts for the rarity of variances among the different recensions). This meant that the knowledge of such a tradition could no longer be a matter of having a rough idea of what tradition consisted of and then draw from that inheritance's material for free elaboration and transmission. The whole matter having become a fixed patrimony, there was no other way left but to commit the whole body to memory. At this point, however, the amount of verses, come down from immemorial times and divided in different lores for the purpose of their ritual use; their explanations and interpretations as found in the Brahmanas, together with their philosophical inner meaning worked out in the Aranyakas and Upanishads; and the rules put down regarding those rites in the Sutras, had become so extensive that it was humanly impossible to be handled by a single group of individuals (even if extremely skilled). The solution was found in fragmentation, in the same way as the cultural and social framework of this variously articulated population was segmented in castes and classes, with stages in life growth and aims to attain, in order paradoxically to preserve its basic unity. Accordingly, the 'texts', starting from the hymns collected in Samhitas (Collections) and continuing with their attached Brahmanas, with their sub-divisions in Aranyakas and Upanishads, and matching Sutras, were divided in four groups, with ritualistic preeminence given to three of them leaving out the fourth consisting of the texts belonging to the Atharvan Brahmins, and each of those groups allotted to a set of priests (theoretically) charged with special tasks in the performance of a Yajna: mainly those trusted with the manual work involved in the rites and those in charge of the recitation or chant of selected hymns according to the offerings and other sacrificial instances, taken from their allotted groups.

Given this somewhat anomalous situation, in what follows we are forced to take up the two subject matters together, trying to maintain as far as possible a kind of structural order. And so we start by presenting the priests, who were divided into four orders or categories so as to match their respective duties. Perhaps these categories were not yet so differentiated in the early Vedic times and the priest in charge of the manual actions was also engaged in composing new hymns for the Deity concerned, at least as far as it can be assumed through some hints scattered here and there in the earliest Rigvedic Mandalas.[24] This 'specialization' became, however, a must when sedentary life revealed the complexity of a differentiated type of life in a different set up brought down to society in a way that had to be tamed and reduced again into liveable terms. Not a little share in this need of specialization and division of ritual duties was taken by the necessity of memorizing to perfection a huge bulk of fixed knowledge, a strain which was further enhanced by the difficulties of having to deal at the same time with a variety of ritualistic subtleties.

i) The Priests

Accordingly, we find the priestly class divided into four groups, always somehow respecting the 3+1 scheme, consisting of:

a). The Adhvaryus, in charge of the factual work of all the manual necessities, including also the recitation of those pertinent hymns attached to his portion of the Vedas: the Yajur. (See later). Other three helpers may assist him: names? Since the texts this category is connected to are divided, as we shall see below, into different Schools, also its members are equally divided in at least four branches, two of which are the most important: the followers of the Madyandina School of the White (Shukla) Yajurveda mostly alive in North India, and those of the Taittiriya School of the Black (Krishna) Yajurveda, still prospering in the South of India. Both stand for the greatest majority of Brahmins today.

b). The Hotar, connected with the Rigveda, whose mantras he has to recite at given moments in any Sacrificial Performance. He also can be assisted by three helpers: Brahmins belonging to this category are rare today and they seem to be on the wane, though not as much as those pertaining to the following one,

c'). The Udgatar, These are dealing with the chanting of the Samaveda, and their decline in number is attributed to the fact that this category is the only one whose members are not appointed officially by a Yajamana when starting preparation for a Yajna. The Udgatar appears on the scene by himself, and this fact seems to have hampered the necessity of his very presence on the required spot. He too could rely on the support of three helpers:

d). The fourth category, perhaps the +1 of the series, belongs to the Atharvaveda, whose texts seem to have been accepted rather late in the network of recitation in Yajna[25]. He also is helped by his own three assistants, thus making the presence of the priests to reach the round figure of 16, the cube of the basic number representing the Earth, but having always in mind that three had to stand against an added one—the three representing Heaven, or the celestial vault, or even the Divine Masculine Principle opposed to the Feminine Earthly element. To this round (perfect) number occasionally is added a seventheenth priest as an overall supervisor. Also this priest is supposed to belong to the Atharvaveda's group. His peculiar task puts him in the position of mastering the whole sacrificial scenery and background, thus giving him the possibility both: to detect errors and mistakes and therefore also the possibility to atone for them with special rites, *prayaksit*; and to have such a complete view of the whole panorama as to enable him to mould its content. This is, possibly, the distant cause for the fact that it has fallen to the specimen of this very class the responsibility to form the link between this deeply rooted culture and spirituality with its popular expression, as manifested in the Epics and the Puranas—as we are going to see in the next chapter. In so far, then, as the main assets of the 'new' religion in its popular form are formally referred to as connected with the Atharvan tradition, the representatives of this category should be almost numberless; actually, however, this branch of Brahmins nowadays counts rather few members.

ii) The Texts

Now that we come at last to the task of presenting the Sacred Lore or the Sacred (oral) Literature, most of its names and ritual purposes have been already mentioned and explained several times by now. Nevertheless, it is not too out of place altogether to go over them once more and try to give a systematised look to the whole bulk in its several divisions, both on an horizontal plane: i.e., its fourfold branches; and in its vertical dimension: i.e., its fourfold division in content.

To begin with, we have to state again that 'Yajnic' ceremonies went through a sharp increase in dimensions and complexity when they had to extend their means in order to cover every possible aspect and nuance of new living situations. Literature dealing with the topic, consequently, expanded into new hymns and explanatory formulas, thus adding the Corpus of the Yajurveda to the ancient hymns, now in need of rearrangement into well defined Collections, Samhitas, in order to facilitate their use during recitation, and also to be correlated with an explanatory literature, the Brahmanas.

Thus, this sacred literature is not only divided horizontally into four groups, but follows also a so to say 'vertical' division, each portion consisting of:

1. A Collection of Hymns, Samhita,

2. A Corpus of related instructions, Brahmanas, explaining and commenting upon the use of such hymns in the sacred performance, completed with myths, and with interpretations concerning their tasks and results. A full veritable cultural and philosophical World-view is presented in this fashion, together with appropriate cosmologies and cosmogonies differing among themselves according to the rituals they are attached to.

This Corpus, with the dropping rate of actual sacrificial performances and consequent deepening of abstract reflections meant to squeeze and pull out all the hidden implications of the described Yajnas, soon stood in need of new sections more clearly connected with mental involvement. They were somehow separated from the main bulk of the Brahmanas as such and referred to as:

3. Aranyakas, that is, 'speculations pursued in hermitages placed in the forest—Aranyaka actually meaning "belonging to Forest". In the reported discussions going on amongst the sages about some particularly important ritual items, the widespread tendency of the speakers is to consider and extract the spiritual implications hidden in gestures, recitations, actions, postures and related items.

Finally an additional portion is further separated from the whole, creating a new division formed by the most philosophical chapters generally the lasts of the entire source-Brahmana. They are, in fact, called also, complexly, Veda-anta, that is the End of the Vedas. This new part is the:

4. Upanishads—a term variously explained but usually derived from Up and Nish and taken to signify "sitting at the feet (of the gurus)"—the more spiritual of the whole lot, whose connection with the original Sacrifice becomes thinner and thinner. Virtually, the ancient Sacred Action, if ever mentionned at all, is totally internalized and its results sublimized and transferred to the effects that the knowledge of its various items can

produce to the meditating subject through his identification with the 'supernatural' object of his reflection.

Horizontally, this fourfold division (in which the Upanishads for their 'otherworldly' shift take the role of the +1) is reproduced in all the four Vedas mentionned above, which are, in their traditional order:

1. Rigveda, containing the most ancient Mantras handed down by tradition (at least from the point of view of their content) and arranged, perhaps at the time of the final redaction of all cultural items, to be fitted into proper recitation in Yajnas. Its Samhita, i.e. Collection, is divided, in one tradition, into ten books or Mandalas, whose central ones (from 2 to 7) assemble the hymns according to the families of the main Rishis, or Poets[26], while the eighth and the ninth are formed by the hymns pertaining to special Soma sacrifices, and the first and the tenth are made up of the more recent issues and are more philosophical in nature. The whole Rigveda forms the portion assigned to the priest called Hotar for recitation in a Yajna. It was later correlated with two Brahmanas, when explanations became necessary: the Aytareya and the Kausitaki/Sankhayana.

2. Samaveda, made up mostly by the same hymns as the preceding group, but arranged in a special way to suit a more elaborate manner of chanting, and are the portion of the priest Udgatar. Its Brahmanas are the most numerous of the lot.

Judging from the content of the hymns and their ancient language, vibrating with a powerful sound, the mantras of these two groups of Samhitas, together with those of the Atharvaveda, belonged to a far away Past almost faded into a 'mythical' lost perfection and in a strong need to be recovered and incorporated again in the emerging Present. Only if we consider them as a recovered fading tradition, revitalized in a new capacity as a powerful Word difficult to be handled and once very effective when created or heard by their inspired poets-seers; as a Sound very important for its forceful vibrations—but less for the meaning it carries along; and as a strong Memory of a previous condition, which, indeed because "previous" therefore "lost", has to be kept alive for maintaining an ideal continuation with a Present in transformation so that has to be fixed again into a new mould, we can conciliate the 'scholarly' historical view with the traditional feeling that, in spite of the oldness of the 'world' depicted in the hymns, they are actually dependent on their Brahmanas, which represent a rather more recent social situation.

3. The Yajurveda is, indeed, the Veda of the 'settled' generation, directly furnished with explanatory Brahmanas from the start. It belongs to the priest Advaryur entrusted with the carrying on of the actual sacred

performance and therefore the most important of them all. The proof of such importance is given by the fact that, unlike the descendants of the Udgatar and of the Hotar, his own descendants form the majority of the existing Brahmans today, as just seen. Most prominent are, especially, those belonging to the Madyandina School of the White Yajurveda more common in the North of the country and those pertaining to the Taittiriya School of the Black Yajurveda in the South. Its Brahmanas, few in number, are divided into its two main Branches: the Shukla or White and the Krishna or Black, each divided at its turn into several schools: Madyandina, and Kanva for the former and Taittiriya, Kathaka, Maitrayani, Kapisthala, for the latter. The vibratory force of its Sound is by far the strongest of the four.

The fourth of the group, somehow separated from the rest because its mantras are not normally used in the Yajnas and his priest plays rather the role of silent supervisor, is the:

4. Atharvaveda, containing the hymns of the Atharvans, similar in mood and content to those of the Rigveda, though some of them are more explicitly magic spells, while others reveal a high philosophical standard[27] This Veda has only one Brahmana attached to it, the Gopatha, while its priests are on the fading line like the Hotar and the Udgatar when considered in their purely classical lineage, however their culture is the matrix out of which, as we have seen and shall see soon, the new 'popular' Hinduism has spread.

c. Shift of emphasis: interiorization and switching from ritual action to ritual knowledge.

As just seen, this cosmology was thought about, devised, built up and transmitted to memory in a well organized sacred literature, during very important yet also very sporadic sacrificial sessions. In those sessions, certain acts were supposed to be performed while selected priests enhanced those acts' strength and efficacy through the power of recited hymns. In this way they set in motion a current of sacred energy able to stir the Divine Energy at large, of which the Yajnic is but a counterpart, helping it in its growth and causing it, therefore, to be available for producing the desired results. At the same time, the whole ritual procedure enabled the gathering of huge crowds of spectators, distinguished guests and learned people, just providing during the long gaps between a rite and another the proper milieu and occasion for high scholarly discussions among experts between themselves in order to solve the not rare liturgical impasses, and for the sake of instructing the high caste members gathered there.

However, the rarity itself of such occasions served also as a spur to find some alternative ways of maintaining constant the energy's flux between this world and the Universe and to keep things going on smoothly even without its supporting rites. It seemed that a difficult situation had aroused. In order to adequately extol sacrifice in the eyes of possible sponsors, the astounding statement was pronounced that "if the priest (on behalf of the sacrificer) did not celebrate the Agnihotra (a offering of hot milk on the sacrificial fire, in mornings and evenings during an allotted time liable to stretch also for several years, but also for much shorter periods) the sun would not rise" (SatBr II.3 1 5), a statement that fully matched the dimension of Yajna. In practice, however, the priests themselves were aware of the fact that, for most of the time, there were no sponsors readily available to carry on such an important performance[28].

A similar situation presented itself to another religion, very different in many a respect from that of the Vedics: Judaism. And, in spite of being worlds apart in their respective cults, in their conceptions of the Divine and of the ensuing cosmologies and cosmogonies, the direction of their theorical way out of ritualistic impact was rather similar. This consideration helps to pinpoint the fact that even in religion—a realm that 'scientific' minded people are inclined to confine into the 'imaginary' and therefore not subjected, as other items falling under the domain of experiments, to the same rules of 'objectivity' and of 'cause and effect' reactions—there is a similar chains of ideas when they are evolving through reasoning over homologous practical or theoretical points of departure. The Hebrews, like practically all the people following theistic beliefs, bestowed great importance to sacrifices, especially those officially performed by the state authorities on behalf of the nation and of the people as a whole. But, whilst amongst the Romans, for instance, or the Greeks, or the Etruscans, etcetera, every city, town, village, and city quarter had its temple or even temples in which divine services were regularly getting on side by side the main services performed by the state authorities in the main temple or in the king's palace, whereas the Hebrews concentrated their state's sacrificial cult on a single spot: the Temple of Jerusalem. This forced them to find some kind of daily or weekly or monthly substitute in all the other cities of their nation, where places of prayers, the Synagogues, were built instead of temples so as to enable those responsible for religious services and instructions to provide their charges with a dealing in common with the 'other-world' and to maintain a kind of regular contact with their God.

Failing the actual participation in the main cult going on only in the capital of the kingdom, the Holy Scriptures were read and explained in all their possible and pertinent meanings, and prayers were conveniently recited, while a good deal of emphasis was also put on moral and social conduct. This scheme turned out to be very useful later on when Jerusalem was conquered and its Temple totally destroyed; people's minds and behaviours were already accustomed to consider their main cultic act more as a theory than a real practice—except of course for the main priests in charge of the Temple and the people going there in pilgrimage to attend some of the important festivals. And when that Temple was no longer there, it was not difficult to achieve total independence from ritual actions in the relationship of God with his chosen people. A similar event had occurred in their history some 500 years before with the destruction of the same Temple at the hands of the Mesopotamians, and the consequent exile of the elite to Babylon. An internalised worship continued, together with the very existence of God himself and the meaning of the forcibly interrupted sacrifices was preserved and enlarged through regular recollection of their ritualistic details. When centuries later the Hebrews were allowed to go back to their Promised Land and to build again their Temple, they were able to take over again their rituals where they had left them, while in addition they had acquired a complete Corpus of Holy Scriptures where their own history was related, together with all procedures for ensuring continuation in worship and in the main cult. When Romans destroyed again and in a definite way the city and the Temple, starting the scattering of the Jews all over the world, the historical period when sacrifices were possible began to be looked upon as the 'perfect standard' and acquired the halo of a kind of 'lost paradise'—lost, as it were, for the second time after Adam's fall—while, at the same strike, all the responsible priestly authorities became busy on two different lines: on one side, to submit sacrifice to a thorough scrutiny in order to extract all its sap, meaning, scope, purposes and effects; and then, on the other, to apply and transfer whatever conclusions they came upon to other possible substitutive actions and means. Prayers, assisted by proper postures, gestures, and a minimal of Liturgical support became prominent in their gathering in Synagogues and other halls; together with recitation and explanation of the Scriptures. A great emphasis was also put on moral conduct and social behaviour together with the observance of Commandments, which became the leading ritual tenets. Oral prayers to their God, maintaining fidelity to Him, and the Sound of liturgical sacred verses, were after the Diaspora the main items that kept Israel united and contributed to reflect and transpose such unity right to the core of the Divinity as such. Abstract thinking where actual practice was out of question afforded a much broader religious and spiritual vision, entailing a deep transformation in the very core of Man and its World-view[29].

The same happened among the Vedic sages, though their social and political situations were much less dramatic. Actually, they were historically at their best, at their acme; but during the process of settling down, as seen, there were less compelling occasions for which such difficult and exacting Sacred Actions were absolutely required...and without any real vital need many expected Yajamanas shrank from the prospect of getting involved in it. Apart the enormous amount of riches squandered around, since, in spite of cosmic and cosmological implications, the whole thing was rather based on personal necessities, the sacrificer had to be individually fitted for the task, living a pure life up to the sacrificial standard, and submitting himself—together with his main wife—to very severe austerities. Accordingly, who could be found pious enough, or 'crazy' enough, to agree in venturing forth for such harsh proposals if not somebody driven by the dire necessity of having a male son not coming in a spontaneous way[30], or pushed by a proud urge of boosting his glory and political power before neighbouring nations? Few indeed. For the rest, priests and specialized Brahmins were more or less in the same position of the Hebrew Rabbis in provincial towns in Israel or, later, in the Diaspora, without even a Temple to refer to. No wonder that, almost since the beginning of their being worked out, the rules of cult took more to the abstract than to actual application. Soon the repeated formula stating the importance of pertinent knowledge of all the details of Sacrifice as the irreplaceable means to get full results from the performance itself became the leading steps toward substituting inner deep understanding to actual gestures, offerings and similar paraphernalia. To know the inner meaning of rituals soon amounted to become those meaning, thus giving rise to a most involving procedure of establishing correspondences between the Divine macrocosms and the human microcosms, as a preliminary to a subsequent merging of the two in an encompassing Reality in which everything is seen in its intrinsic Unity.

However, this push toward the importance of knowledge for fostering a spiritual transformation of any microcosm into its corresponding macrocosm, could not erase all traces of cultic lingering, especially when occasional powerful kings—as history and Epics confirm—were still stimulated into exhibiting in this way their political achievements or when, in a more modest fashion, ordinary people with no special inclination for mysticism wanted still to get Yajna's benefits, without being, at the same time, totally plunged into Action, either because unwilling to get themselves involved with ascetic discomfort or more often because not entitled to perform them directly. The way out, like among the Hebrews, was found in the recitation of the texts theoretically involved in the various kind of Yajnas, without the botheration of further involvements: a recitation, of course, implying a proper training, the right pitch of voice, perfect modulation together with correct pronunciation and especially the rendering of the powerful vibrations contained in the mantras, so as to acquire the inner strength proper to rite. In this way, the force of Sound took over above other ritualistic considerations and, already from rather ancient time, became the main substitute for obtaining physical and spiritual desires and results. When to the consciousness of those who got the authority over such matters Sound became the most powerful means to obtain results, even above the elusive solemn performances, a related process of deepened comprehension was soon set in motion and the oral Sacred Texts became to yield to meditations on them and to 'reveal' different layers of their understanding.

During the process of replacing complicate ceremonies with a rather simpler recitation the task of adjustment had to work on two levels: to transfer and concentrate the power of a very complex action to a disembodied Sound, and then to provide it with something tangible again so as to furnish it once more with a kind of ritual presentation by which people still under the pressure of their senses could feel the difference between a simple narration and a ritualistic display of powerful Sounds. Recitation, then, became shrouded again in a kind of ritual procedure, requiring proper postures, right frame of mind, appropriate gestures of fingers, hands and arms (mudras)—at least in the Vedic Schools of North India—and occasionally also in the presence of an enkindled flame, in order to provide the setting for a kind of coming back of the suppressed ritual Fire[31].

Yet this recitation, concentrating as it were directly on Sound rather than on meaning, soon lost sight of the latter—which in any case was getting more and more obsolete since with the elaboration of rites, first, and, then, with their gradual sinking into a supporting theoretical background, the very concept of the related Divine figures and expressions also were submitted to a slow but intensive change[32]—and new levels of comprehension were disclosed to the ever attentive priests and sages. Once again this further classification followed the same mandalic scheme of the well-known 3+1. Actually such levels of understanding are recognized for their value as applicable to all systems of language; they are: 1ˢᵗ the Level of overt communication of a content, vaikhari; 2ⁿᵈ the Intermediary Level, that of Song and Mind, madhyama; 3ʳᵈ the Intuitive Level or level of Vision, pasyanti; with the addition of the 4ᵗʰ. The Level of Eternity or have Creative Silence, Para (the one beyond).

The domain of the literal content, the story, the one presenting the Divinity that has to be worshiped and the related modality of such worship, belongs to the first layer, the vaikhari. The second level, madhyama, is reached when the emphasis of recitation is shifted to the modulation of the voice, even to the point of tuning the verses to a chant, involving the mental processes with the deeper emphasis on the ensuing vibrations: the carriers of ritual power and energy. These two levels, being somehow more reachable, are those that can be deemed appropriate, the first for the lay person who can only grasp the obvious, and the second for the Brahmachary who learns especially the right tune and the perfect pronunciation of the sound beyond the actual meaning. Such meaning is not disclosed to him because it is considered cumbersome and with distracting effects from the perfection of vocalization; this second level is also that shared by the householder, the Grhasta, who wishes his priests to recite the Veda for his welfare and that of his wife. The third level goes further down in the depths of understanding and discloses flashes of Intuition over the more profound spiritual Realities; people already on their spiritual path, the Vanaprasthas and especially the Sanyasis, reach it occasionally. But only a really 'realized soul' is able to penetrate the 4ᵗʰ level of Creative Silence, the "Beyond" par excellence. It is in the 3ʳᵈ level that sages have perceived, in flashing lights, the Divine dimension of the Word, the Sound vibrating and reverberating into Infinity, connected with the Eternity of the Absolute, and seen by the sages as Self-existing, i.e., "without author", apauruseya; in the 4ᵗʰ even that kind of perception no longer exists and Silence can only be experienced by letting oneself being absorbed by It. From this Primordial Silence, "beyond even Being and Non-Being", as a Vedic mantra (RV X.129.1) puts it, Word stirred up first through an initial vibration produced at the beginning of Time by a hidden internal Desire (kama) and then achieved by an act of Self-heating (tapas), (Ib.2ff).

Thus, this accomplishment of the sages, brought about by personal ascent into the unspeakable heights of the Divine, of the Absolute, coupled with a subsequent descent in their effort to translate that supreme experience in terms graspable by thought and expressible in an understandable language, can be attributed to their attempt to overcome the necessity of performing rites that had no longer proper occasions to be regularly carried on. However, this very necessity worked also in an opposite direction, not so much as a spur for launching sages soaring into Infinity than as a mean for forcing them into finding also a substitute for rituals at the level of common, uninitiated, people. This need to adapting a World-view originally conceived to fit a rather homogeneous population, as already seen, to a much wider range of people where specialization in trade and walks of life added further differences to an enlarged average folk, probably began to be felt when Sacred Knowledge shifted from actual Actions, automatically selecting its participants, to the easiest device of recitation.

The discovering of so many levels in the Words themselves, with a connected difficulty of grasping their profound significance, immediately made sages aware of a new problem: the damage that could ensue to such very Knowledge by an undue spreading among people who could not be in the position to share its deep meaning. After all, what is attained through a profound type of meditation and experience cannot be even imagined by those who did not have direct experience of it or even did not have inner disposition for such insights. Thus, since by not understanding them these people could distort the message and the Truth realised through a very hard-worked intuition, it was imperative to protect such Truth and the means used to reach it. Secrecy slowly began to creep in around all that 'smelt' of Vedas; only those who belonged to the three high castes could approach this religious culture without danger for themselves. The fear of having the Sacred Efficacy spoiled by misunderstanding, turned Vedic Knowledge into a menace for the integrity of the unprepared person so that the Secrecy, by which it started to be surrounded with, was justified by the implication that the power arising from ritual recitations would be lethal for those unprepared to stand it. And this, actually, appears to be a real fact on both levels: the people not having had any experience of this sort could not understand its deep meaning so that they would degrade it to 'nonsense', while those who could intuit it in spite of their lack of adequate preparation could be psychologically shaken by the inseparability of a sudden frightening 'revelation' of an Impersonal, Infinite and Eternal Absolute peering out beyond a non-understandable Sound. Thus, it soon became clear that that feeling of danger of pollution has to be extended on equal ground even to the ordinary members of the 'fitted' castes, who could also pollute or misinterpret[33] or be frightened by ritual issues if not adequately spiritually hardened by ascetic discipline and exercises[34]. They too, if not properly prepared, could not stand the power of Vedic recitation, nor could face the depth of their more esoteric levels.

Hence the mistrust still lingering up to the present day about the 'uncunning' tendency of the Brahmins to "keep for themselves" those "powerful tools", little knowing about the price these 'specialists of the Sacred' had to pay in asceticism and worldly detachment; neither do they want to be aware that, in any case, such 'Power' would continue to elude them because it is placed on a different ground of comprehension altogether.

But, then, how to comply, in religious matters, with the justifiable needs of unfitted ordinary caste people, the vast number of the Sudras and all the female folk (both groups being considered 'unfitted' par excellence)? And here is where the so-called 'popular religion' has its stand.

o*o*o*o

However, before shifting to another chapter in order to present such religion properly, a purely mechanical dilemma arises in the procedure. Having come out with the problem of the esoteric Secrecy surrounding Vedic lore, the obvious continuation that suggests itself is its counterpart: the exoteric, popular, religion springing out from the deep Truth but rendered reachable to everybody's imagination and understanding. Yet, this Vedic exposition had up to now dealt especially with the practical side of its cult: its self-supporting sacrificial Action, so complete in itself that it can stand alone as the main pillar of a whole culture, including its philosophical World-view, its social foundations, and its own conception of the Divine. So much so that it had postponed a presentation of that Divine, in its impersonal Absoluteness as well as in its personalized features. Now the two points collide. Thus, in order to preserve a more comprehensible sequence we found more convenient to break the logical succession and shift the treatment of Divine figures, dealt with in the Vedas later on in a separate division, considering them together with those belonging to exoteric believes.

NOTES

1. Perhaps the much quoted sentence of the Master of Nazareth: "give to Cesar....." was a way for keeping his disciples not distracted from the main issue of his preaching: the Freedom of the soul. Only later it became a good expedient to keep medieval Church out of the grips of the Germanic "Roman Empire", though allowing it to have its own political power

2. See, for exhaustive descriptions of the Vedic Yajnas K.R. Potdar, *Sacrifice in the Rig-Veda (its nature, influence, origin and growth)*, Bombay (Bh. Vidya Bhawan), 1953; S.Levi, *La doctrine du sacrifice dous les Brahmanas* reprint Paris (PUF)

1966 (or. 1898) G.U. Thite, *Sacrifice in the Brashmana Texts*, Pune (B.U.P.) 1975; U.M.Vesci, *Heat and Sacrifice in the Vedas*, op. cit; and for comparison with the Greek counterpart W. Burkert. *Homo Necans: Interpretation on Alt griechische Opfer Riten und Mythes*, Berlin, NY (W.de Gruyter) 1972 (there is an Engl. Transl.): M.Detienne, J-P Vernant, *La cuisine du sacrifice en pays grec*. Paris. (P.U.F.), 1979 C Grottaneli, & N.F. Parisi (ed) *Sacrificio e Societa nel mondo antico*, Bari (Laterga) 1988.

3.   See any book on Indian History, as. E.g., K.A.Nilakanta Sastri & G. Srinivasachari, *Advanced History of India*. Bombay (Allied & Publishers)1970, p.33 for early Vedas and pp.48 ff for later Vedas and Brahmanas, where their territories seem to have extended from Gujarat on one side and to the complete Ganga plain on the other.

4.   That is the very reason of the content of the Brahmanas and the Sutras.

5.   See, e.g. Sat Br V,5,4, 25 ff about the Asvins and their myths on their healing power, explaining in some details the hints found in RV X. 131, 4 & 5.

6.   This prospective came to me with discussion with professor A.N.Pandey, in Delhi. Emeritus IIT DELHI

7.   Sat Bz XIV, 1.1.2 makes a specific reference to this place where a main sacrifice was performed. For the importance of this sacred session in the arrangement of the Vedic and Puranic literature see. G. Bonazzoli", "*The Dynamic Canon of the Puranas*," in Puranas 26 (July 1979) and in most of his articles in the same Bulletin from 1975 to 1987.

8.   See my doctoral thesis: "God, Man, Salvation in the spiritual movements of the VI cent BC from China to Greece" (in Italian), Roma (La Sapienza), 1963 [but such waves are found also in the XIII BC or XIII AD etc.]

9.   See Gop. Br I.5.23 ff

10.   See Ait Br II. 3.3

11.   See *Heat & Sacrifice*, op .cit., p.89ff with fotnote18.

12.   See, e.g M.Eliade, *Histoire des croyances et des ideés religienses*, 5 vols, Paris (Payot), 1976 (1984) Vol I (1984) p.233. See also §§, 73-75.

13.   The phrasing of an Indian scholar about such "obligatorily" is revealing "As soon as one set up the sacred fire the Agnihotra became obligatory to him", where the condition is subjected to the starting the sacrificial session , R.N. Sharma, *Culture & Civilization as Revealed in the Shrautasutras*, Delhi, (Nag.Publ.) 1977 p.50 f.

14.   Cf. RV X. 90 and the Upanishads where the theme is recurrent (See. S.Radhakrishnan, ed.)

15.   See. e.g. Sat Br XII. 8.3.14.

16.   See J G Fraser Th Golden Bough 3rd in 12 volumes 1911-1915 (combined into a single volume.

17.   See Fr. Stall Agni, op.cit.

18.   See later on.

19.   Quotation from R.Panikkar, *Myth, Faith, Hermeneutics*, NY (Pauhst Pr) 1979, p.74. See Sat Br III, 9.1.1.ff; PancBr XXV. 17.3 ff; etc for textual references.

20.   See references in Grihya Sutras, Vol XXIX and XXX of Sacred Books of the East N.Delhi Motilal Banarasidas, Indian Ed 1967

21.   See any treatise on Comparative Religion as, e.g., M.Eliade, *Histoire de croyances religiouses*, op.cit, all 3 vols issued; W.Burkert, *Homo Necans*, op. cit, etc

22.   See e.g.,Van Der Leeuw *Phenomenology of Religion* Tubingen 1956.

23.   I may recollect here a personal experience. At the beginning of my studies in India I asked a learned traditional pandit (scholar) of Lucknow that what was the

difference among the various denominations of the Sacred Scriptures? I wanted to know what differentiated Yajur Veda from. Rigveda or Samveda as texts, and the answer was: "not much, only some rules about their reciprocal availability or refusal of availability in marriages!" To my puzzled enquiry it was explained that he was speaking about the priests belonging to their textual tradition, because for him they were one and the same thing.

24. See e.g. RV II. 2. 13; II. 53, 1.3 V.43.14; V I.23.10 etc.

25. Warrant to this is the frequency of Brahmans names still present today where Tripathi or Tiwaris (referring to affiliation of three Vedas) are more common than Dvivedi or Dube pointing to only two, and than Chaturvedi implying also the addition of the Atharva, the last one.

26. The II belongs to the Rsi Gritsamada; the III to Rsi Visvamitra (and contains the most famous verse called the Gayatri, important daily Prayer for Brahmans (III. 62.10); IV mostly to Gautama Vamadeva; the V to Atri and the Atreyas; the VI to Bharadvaja; the VII to Vasista (the rival of Visvamitra).

27. See, for instance, AV, X.2 dealing with Purusa (the Primordial Man), or X, 7 describing the Cosmic Pillar (Skandha); XX.53 dedicated to Time (Kāla); etc.

28. See Sat Br II 3.1.13.

29. See a description of such move towards the universalization and spiritualization of the Divine in Israel and in other religions as well in my doctoral thesis "God, Man, Salvation". op. cit.

30. As, for instance, in the Ramayana where the King of Ayodhya has to perform one in order to have a male child and get four of them from his three wives.

31. I, personally, took part in two such occasions: in the first (in a private house in Varanasi, in the middle'70s) the recitation of the four Vedas was carried on by four priests inside the premises, without fire; in the second [in an Ashram—Monastery/Convent—on the mountains (c/o Pilot Baba in 1990)]. a Sacred fire was burning and receiving oblations.

32. We shall come back to it in the next ch. pt, where shall be seen how the concept of the Divine changed from the early Vedic personal figures, to the more abstract personification of the Sacrificial Action itself into the Godhead Prajapati in the Brahmanas, up to the totally abstract idea of Brahman, the Absolute, in the Upanishads: but also to come back again in the personalized Entities of the Pauranic Deities.

33. And here I cannot refrain from reporting the unbalancing factor of my very presence in a modern sacrificial performance, occurring in Varanasi about 35 years ago. On the basis that I was a "Vedic Scholar" I was allowed to assist at such ceremony; but the Yajamana got grey with fear when he found out that I was an impure not vegetarian.

34. This effect has been reported—in a different milieu and in a different situation—by C.G.Jung, about a man, who wanting to kill himself for love disappointment, witnessed, from the bridge where he was standing, a most remarkable vision of a Starry sky reflected in the moving water. As Jung remarked, he was blown out by a vision which could inspire a stronger soul into poetry or mysticism.

CHAPTER 2
Popular religion

Now, Vedic religion, turning, as just seen, on itself and becoming more and more interiorised into a 'specialised' matter—'specialised' in so far as, in order to be able to 'hear' the Cosmic Sound the Vedas have become, one must have developed a 'special' understanding amounting to Sanctity—slowly withdrew from the common people's reach and sunk into a cultural background faintly perceived as the all-supporting foundation of the entire religious edifice, and therefore, as all foundations are, quite invisible and unapproachable. Only the priests, the Purohitas, were familiar with its intricacies and even the few Yajamanas who consented to be dragged in a Yajnic performance depended *in toto* from the knowledge of their priests, mechanically repeating the mantras they were asked to repeat and faithfully copying the gestures they were required to do and were shown how to do.

But if this was the situation, it was soon clear that something had to be done in order to cover the religious needs and requirements of the vast masses, including those caste members (and they were by now the most numerous) who, though allowed to share the high doctrines, were neither interested at nor properly committed to or innerly fit for them—in ancient times as well and not only today. It was imperative, therefore, that the whole lore of Vedic Knowledge, the Wisdom of the Fathers, with its conceptions of Divine figures, its rituals, its 'specialised' World-views, had to be thought over again and formulated anew so as to be presented under expressions more suitable to the times and to the ordinary level of the average population. This task traditionally has fallen upon the shoulders of the members of the Atharvavedic line, the ones, as seen, who in the sacrificial economy of a theoretical performance were supposed to supply the Silent Supervisor, the Brahman. Such a position allowed these priests to acquire, over generations, a global vision of the entire culture, with its subtleties together with its widest range, in a way that made them fit to extract the juice, *rasa*, of the whole World-view not so much in flashes of inner intuitive light for their own benefit but in order to translate it into new images of the Divine with more appeal to popular imagination. The resulting narrations, either in the form of Epics—that is, taking their characters from prototypes of historical events—or straight in the manner of 'myths'—that is, with the direct involvement of Divine figures—were also collected into a Religious Corpus (possibly during the same Sacrificial Session that saw the final organization of Vedic literature, or during a contemporary connected Yajna in a not too far away locality—Kurukshetra for the first and Naimisaranya for the second) and committed to the recitation and interpretation of priests, though by now writing them down for recording is not only allowed but become a meritorious act.

a. The texts

The new 'sacred literature' is somehow much lighter in mood and, though undoubtedly soon raised to the heights of truly religious support, never reached the level of the Vedas even in the eyes of its followers. It was called, however, the Fifth Veda, a designation held in common with the Agamas, the Tantric Literature, and from the Vedas inherited the function of forging and supporting a new cultural and religious world-view in a lighter and more understandable way of presenting, interpreting and living the Divine.

Essentially such literature consisted of two main Epics, centred on the lives and exploits of some heroes who in due time turned into veritable Gods—or at least were absorbed by one of the two main Deities as His "descents" or "incarnations", *avataras*—and of a group of Traditional Tales, called Puranas, (perhaps "Old lores" since in Sanskrit purana means "old", "ancient"), describing the characters, personalities and events of Gods, in their turn 'mythic' personifications of the Ultimate Divine realized by the Vedic intuition and worked out by later philosophical speculations. The Puranas soon grew steadily into fairly good numbers arranged by Tradition into a standard number of eighteen Major Purana (Mahapuranas) and an equal number of Minor Puranas (Upapuranas); not always, however, there is agreement among Pauranic sources themselves on the titles making up the two groups, thus leaving somehow open the conjecture that originally the Puranas were more and got organized only in a second time, around a different significance of their number.

Due, perhaps, to the fact that, as seen, the Vedic world-view slowly sang too deep in the whole cultural consciousness (thus remaining alive hardly for a thin group of 'specialists'), the Epic and Pauranic literature, more at the level of common comprehension and easily translatable into pious models to be followed and copied by devotees in their own behaviours, in due time took over the cultural and religious role first played by the Vedas. More or less around the centuries immediately before and after the Christian era during the rise of great kingdoms like those of Mauryas and, later, of Guptas aiming at imperial domination, the Pauranic world is found convenient for moulding the people's behaviour and consciousness. Their texts, accordingly, become widely known, devotedly listened to, together with explanations going side by side with the recitation as still witnessed in temples and Ashram gatherings; while temples were erected around the figures, murtis, of these 'new' Gods and Goddesses. In fact, the event of the Pauranic and Epic Divinities imposing themselves to the devotional mood of people—as we are going to see later when dealing with the Divine aspect of religion—brought with it an entire change in the outlook of worship, introducing new methods different from Yajnic types; the most striking difference being in the fact of not involving fire, but of concentrating efforts and interest on the external forms of such Divinities. The texts dealing with this kind of cult, explaining its mode and way of execution, and enlarging their range to include the 'sacraments', (samskaras), fostering human growth and change of status, have to be extracted from Pauranic and Epic literatures and selected for the purposes according to the examples settled by Gods, Goddesses, Heroes and human prototypes. On them and on the need to find a kind of correspondence with the overall Vedic lore, precipitated at the bottom (to use a chemical image) but certainly not forgotten, a huge Corpus of Doctrines and Rules, called Dharma Sastras, grew to fix and delineate the behavioural and ritualistic codes with the aim of rooting again all this mushrooming Divine expressions into the Vedic solid cultural ground.[1]

In presenting here the texts in a slightly more detailed way it occurs straight away that the Vedic 'mandalic' structure of a fourfold division, based on the 3+1 pattern, is here lost into an explosion of multiplicity, rearranging itself into the first multiple of 9 (the number that could well represent the shifting mood of creation: a multiplicity always coming back to its main unit and remaining equal to zero in the inner sum of any cipher): 18 which is the worked out standard number of the two main groups of Puranas. The Epics, however, are two as already pointed out and somehow show a kind of very loose resemblance with the Epics of the Greek world: Iliad and Odyssey, which provided the basic texts for the Greek Pantheon in more or less the same way in India they provided the background for the

Hindu one. Such resemblance dwells mainly on the fact that the first of Indian Epic, Ramayana, (like its Greek counterpart: the Odyssey) is centred on the life and adventures of one Hero, Rama, even if he was the first of four brothers and so connected with his wife as to form a kind of worshiping unit; while the second Epic, the Mahabharata, deals (like the—Greek Iliad) with a choral war where the whole of the Indian aristocracy was engaged to his own destruction.[2]

More specifically, Ramayana narrates the whereabouts of its main Hero, Ramachandra (called Rama), the elder son of the king of Ayodya, who was sent into exile for 12 years in the forest, accompanied, on their own accord, by his wife and one of his brothers. From there some 'evil' king of the furthest South snatched away Sita, the hero's wife, and held her prisoner in his royal palace in the island of Shri Lanka, his kingdom beyond the sea. The second part of the narration concerns the search and location of Sita, the preparation of the war against 'evil' and the final conquest and destruction of the enemy with the liberation of the abducted bride. But, once everything is completed and Rama is back again in his kingly position that was his by birthright, He yields to the pressure of his subjects objecting about the supposed lost purity of his wife—a purity essential for the welfare of the whole kingdom—and sent her away to his Guru's Ashram. Here, however, he occasionally visited her since two children were born to them...though as Ashram inmates and not with royal rights. Sita's place as queen needed for the performance of the coronation's rite, Rajasuya, is taken by her effigy as a golden statue. The whole account is presented as "coming to the mind" of its author, Valmiki, and settled in a way as to represent the Divine intervention to cope with Evil in this world[3]. Much later, during the period of a surge of Devotional movement around the XII and XIIIth Centuries of our Era, a well-known poet from Varanasi, Tulsidass, framed again the old Epic and totally divinised his Hero, Rama, as a pure and loyal kind of counterpart to the popularity of Krishna, the Hero of the other Epic and the major protagonist of a dubious nature in many a Purana. Thus Rama became another direct incarnation of Vishnu as the model of virtues and of all perfections. The end is also changed and Sita, after proving her full innocence and purity through a fire ordeal, is reinstalled to her rightful place, at least till the Earth, considering her mission accomplished, raises to swallow her again.

The other Epic, the Mahabharata, is, as stated, a choral work focussed on the main war staged between the members of a royal family, wherein two groups of brothers, cousins to each other, fought for the conquest of the kingdom of their fathers. But actually, around such a seemingly "family matter", the whole Indian aristocracy seem to have joined in the battle-ground, taking parts according to their respective sense of duty, or of affection for one or the other parties involved, or for convenience. The participation of the entire aristocracy, in fact, was supposed to be so thorough that it entailed at the end of the war the total destruction of the Kshatriya caste as a whole. Whatever is found today under such heading is considered to be a new type of extraction altogether. The entire plot is dominated by the figure of Krishna, the king of Dwarka but also the eighth 'incarnation' of Vishnu, or rather Vishnu himself in whole his majesty assuming the figure of a king acting as charioteer for the purpose of leading the "good party" to its victorious achievement—even if not always through the use of straightforward methods. The main gist of the text is the problem that originally arose when the legitimate king, being blind-born, had to leave the throne to his brother, who, in his turn, had to leave the kingdom for reasons of his own. The realm, thus, passed rightfully to his five sons, living together with their mother and their only common wife; while their hundred cousins, sons of the blind king were not pleased with the situation. Through a truly 'Epic' game of dice the eldest of the cousins succeeded, through a ruse, to win from his eldest counterpart the latter's kingdom, his brothers and even their common wife. As a result the five with mother and wife had to leave and remain in exile in the forest for the canonical twelve years plus a thirteenth in disguise, before they could come back to claim their due heritage. They were not detected in their hiding, nevertheless the cousins at the end of the period, refused to comply with their promise. The war, thus, became inevitable and was fanned upon by Krishna himself who, in a famous selected part of the Mahabharata, the Bhagavad Gita (possibly a later addition), persuades a reluctant hero—the third brother on the list—to "perform his Kshtriya duty" and slay his cousins, together with his elders and gurus, because this was Fate's decree. In order to better fostering this persuasion Krishna revealed himself as Vishnu Vishvarupa, the Form of the Universe, and as the Master of all destinies (ch. XI). Yet, although the war was duly fought and won, eventually nobody really could enjoy it benefits. At the end the five winners and Krishna himself quietly either passed away or retired into solitary life[4]. The end of the Epic, together with the end of the original aristocracy, marked also the end of the preceding Yuga and the entrance into the Kali Yuga, our current era, of which Krishna is enthroned as the major Divinity in one of the two major 'Branches' in which Hindu Mythology is divided, as we shall see further down in the chapter devoted to the Divine in Its various forms and shapes.

Krishna, then, as the main Divine Personality of the Kali Yuga, soon became the hero protagonist of a long series of narratives especially dwelling upon his birth, infancy and youth, all marked by an interesting pattern of mischievousness, beginning from his very coming into this world—as a child dreaded by his usurper uncle who tried to suppress him in the same way and in the same line as Zeus was threatened by his father in Greek Mythology and Romulus by his great-uncle in the Roman saga—wherefrom he had to be hidden and snatched away in disguise; continuing with his naughty behaviour as a child among the shepherds where he was concealed, and ending up, as a youth, by playing love with all the female shepherds (the gopis) of the area and weaving a wonderful love-story with Radha, the prototype of deep mystic love, though she was herself a lady married to somebody else (a major sin in Indian society up to nowadays). Such narrations are collected in many of the more important Puranas[5].

Other Puranas deal with the complex and multifarious Divine Personality called Vishnu (of whom Krishna is considered an aspect), and are named after his many different figures or 'descents' (Avataras), including one called after the God's own mount: the Vulture Garuda; while still others focus, instead, on the main Divinity of the second Saga: Shiva, lingering on his character and exploits either alone as an ascetic, as the prototype of ascetics, or sporting with his wife and Shakti (creative Power) who also acts as his pupil. Shiva, however, is not only the main figure of the Puranas concerned with him, but especially is, together with his Feminine Power, the main inspiring divine personality of the vast Tantric literature, consisting of Agamas.

All this variously shaped literature presents a roughly common characteristic: that of dealing with the Divine in a rather 'light' manner, depicting the Deities as a hip of names and forms—the nama-rupa of philosophical tradition—absorbed in and at the same time aloof from the whirling multiplicity of the samsara, the endlessly revolving phenomenical worlds. They are many in their reciprocal relationships and yet they constantly point toward a potential Unity behind their differentiations. Some of the other figures, we are not to deal with here, have also different aspects, some even bordering on the animal species: like Hanuman the Monkey, for instance, or Ganesh with his Elephant head on a child body. Some of the situations created in the narration of Gods' doings can be also hilarious and often members accustomed to the seriousness surrounding especially Monotheistic religions are taken aback by this Indian tendency to laugh at their own more sacred lore. The fact is that subconsciously it cannot easily be forgotten, even if all those Gods and Goddesses have grown into solid Divinities worthy of worship, love and devotion, that their very coming into being was but a product of an exoteric presentation of a Truth, raised to such a sublimation as to become either unreachable to human power or have gone even beyond the task of being conceived; therefore they could not be attained and soiled by any possible laugh or fun. The texts as well as the Murtis further enforce such a joyful attitude, which hints at and betrays a, sound psychological depth in building up mystic growth and religious awareness in communities and individuals alike[6].

Such religious literature, at its turn, though it may appear light to the reader, is, nonetheless, dealing with a new type of presentation of the Supreme Divinities and, therefore, was also made the central referral, as already hinted upon, for a vast exegetical work—somehow equivalent of that raised about the Vedas in the shape of Brahmanas and Sutras—where a good many experienced 'holy' lawyers and sages toiled to cast again their nets of moral, cultural and religious coordinates, fixing once more behavioural measures and either adapting the mythological world to the serious rigidity of Vedic background, or, if one would prefer to see it the other way round, by deeply rooting it into Vedic soil, they provided such a mythological World-view as having a solid grasp into the perfect Past, fashioned by the by-now Divinised Rishis. The result of all these efforts is a substantial bulk of doctrinal and law texts, called, as stated above, Dharma Shastras, whose authorship is given to some of the known Vedic Rishis and masters of the far away Past or, as it seems, to their homonymous descendants. Between them and the Epic and Pauranic religious support, a 'new' code of behaviour and of rites, together with a different way of worship more congenial to Deities exhibiting concrete features and visible images, has been solidly established, especially around the 1st centuries before and after the Christian Era, giving 'new' shapes and interpretations to the old Brahmanic culture. This culture, in fact, was not wiped out but continued, though more as a kind of hidden background than as an open option, side by side to the more appealing 'Hindu' presentation. They were meant to sustain the whole Hindu apparatus in the same manner as the skeleton is the essential support of the whole body. The world-view inspired by the sacred literature just presented will, then, be regarded as the living part of the whole, the flesh and blood, features and expression of a pleasant Reality yet bound to change and fluctuate, contrary to the undecaying but hidden bones' immutable structure.

b. The Rites

All the rites of this so-called 'new era', or 'popular line' of Brahmanic tradition, spring out, naturally, from the new 'mythological' like World-view contained and expressed in the 'new' religious literature. However, the well-woven Brahmanic background continues to surface by furnishing both the models the rituals have to be patterned into and, most of the times, also the texts to be recited during the various performances. In this respect, the rites which are more directly taking their form and inspiration from the 'classical' ones are those marking changes in human conditions, from birth to death passing through coming of age and marriage: the already mentioned samskaras of Indian traditions (called "sacraments" in Christianity so that this noun is also used as a general term applicable to equivalent rites in other religions as well) and also those performed on different occasions as, for instance, the inauguration of a house, the beginning of a new job, the opening or starting of an activity: as trade or teaching or office work and the like.

More in tune with the 'new' religious expressions and mentality are, instead, those rites directly concerned with the worship of the visible Deities and addressed to their Murtis or Images. Even worship, however, may, at its turn, be considered in two sub-divisions, one coming more or less directly from the Vedic practice of reciting the Sacred Texts, the other more specifically devoted to honouring the various Gods and Goddesses concretely made present either in some symbols or in statues and other effigies. This form of homage reserved to the Divine figures had to be necessarily different from the ancient ways of worship because it seems plausible to think that Yajna Actions did not require images in their sacrificial grounds. Not for nothing Yajna bears all the signs of deepening its roots in an ancient nomadic time where a concrete presence of 'idols' was at least encumbering not to say fairly dangerous. Carrying statues or graspable symbols, which could become any moment prey of enemies or of unreliable strange local populations, could not but hamper a fast moving people. The formers, generally belonging to the same stock—as we have seen—could incorporate the Gods and turn their 'protectors' into enemies' allies; the second could simply destroy them, entailing in this way the destruction of the people represented by such idols. The fierce struggle of the Hebrew prophets against any image of their God and for a long time also against the perspective of having a fixed Temple stemmed from the same early cultural background. In their case the sedentary custom slowly took over and a Temple was allowed to be constructed; nevertheless images continued to be forbidden. The Indians, on the whole, were more faithful to their ancestors in the sense that, when the Divine got personalised, the main Gods and Goddesses in whom It revealed itself, though acquiring shapes and images which had to be installed in temples and shrines, did so by keeping the whole issue on a different, yet related, ground and tradition. Thus, when the personalised Deities became visible with names and forms (*nama-rupa*) and in the same act claimed regular worship and proper housing—in temples, shrines and in specially reserved corners of private homes—they did this without interfering with the cultic patterns settled for the Yajna, which still remains basically murti-less. Today, however, images can be installed in a Yajna, in order to please the devotees' piety. But, once there, they remain only superficially connected with what goes on around and in the Sacred Fire. Once there, in fact, such images became in their own right and their own level, the centre of a different cultural homage bestowed on them which included care for the 'idols' in dress and food and presents of various kind. This type of worship, called Puja, differs from Yajna among other things also in the fact that it does not require the presence of Fire. Special proceedings and gestures accompanied with verses and prayers turn the presentation of gifts into a proper ritualistic enterprise, as we are going to see now.

i) Puja

Puja is a worship addressed to a concrete, visible, well-defined Divinity, involving a full care of an image when that image, Murti in Sanskrit, is such that allows for care: cleaning, dressing, feeding; it is also presented with many kind of items among which the light of a pure flame is the best. When the Murti is not a piece of artefact, but a river, a mountain, a tree or other not-anthropomorphic elements, the Puja naturally leaves aside the caring preliminaries, but goes straight to the presentation of offerings, called Bhoga. This type of worship is not a social affair, even if in temples or in private houses its performance can be taken as an excuse for people gathering with the intent of assisting to it and, at the end, of sharing the ensuing "Prasada", that is: "blessed gift from the honoured God or Goddess". The main object of Puja in fact is the Deity itself, and the Pujari— the priest deputed to perform it, who occasionally can also be a female from his family—is reckoned to offer it, just for the sake of the Murti as such, twice a day, morning and evening (in the mornings also in certain occasions completed with the care of the image) with a third optional at lunch time. The performance is more or less standard: the pujari, after completing the preliminary 'toilette' of the images, especially if they are Temple-images (by washing them and rearranging or changing their dresses), squats in front of it and recites the due texts, then he stands and begins the proper offering keeping the presented item in his right hand and holding a little bell in his left. The gift is "shaken"—to take the term from the Hebrews who also speak of "shaking" the offering—with a rotation from left to right in a double circular movement: that of the hand on itself and of the full arm in front of the Deity so as to encircle its figure. This entire rotation is accompanied by the incessant ring of the little bell shaken with a linear movement of the left wrist, rendering the whole exercise rather difficult since it requires a complete independence of the hands. The sound is supposed, like in all cultures, to keep the place free from Demons and other bad spirits—notoriously considered adverse to loud noises—while the circular movement is (perhaps) a transposition into a ritual gesture of the main mark of homage bestow on anything important (from a God to parents, a religious symbol, or a high spiritual or political personality) called "Pradaksina" or "moving around (something) giving it the right". The presentation of the flame, enkindled on a piece of Camphor (the only substance that can burn completely without leaving residual ashes and therefore a suitable symbol for representing total surrender to Divinity) is the last item and the culmination of Puja: it is called Arati.

Most of the times Pujaris, either in temples or in houses, perform their sacred duties in solitude for the sake of the sole Deity, but in those cases where the priest is not alone, as in famous temples or during festival periods, then some assistants enhance the bell tickling with more noisy beating on metallic gongs, blowing conchs and shaking of other type of percussion instruments. Human voices of assistants and, occasionally, of devotees add themselves to the hymns chanted by the Pujari, or, if the latter prefers to mumble his mantras, they contribute to fill the atmosphere to the brim with a more elevating harmony (which in some cases can become also a cacophony) till the abrupt cessation of it all, at the end of the Arati, leaves the presents with a sense of immediate inner void, conducive to a taste of the void experienced in meditation. Personal experience has told me that, though all this is acting at the level of psychological emotion, such noisy performances can be so catching and involving that they may represent a good beginning for a direct inner approach to the Divine.

In India, in fact, all what is social can be individually lived, and, conversely, all that can be considered essentially as an individual reaction can be made into a social matter. A temple's puja of big proportions, as in a crowded Ashram (convent) or in a famous Mandir (temple), can be taken as an example of this kind. In principle one visits a sacred place on a purely individualistic urge (alone or at most with close members of one's family)— often, out of canonical hours, the pujaris are busy just with such type of personal worship and devotion, presenting personal offerings to the Deities and giving back to the donors their deserved Prasada—but when the solemnity of the place or of the time (during daily Arati or during Festivals) gather many people together, then the outburst of high pitched sounds, chants in common and common participation in the Puja may enhance a very emotional surge of psychological power cementing the crowd into a unit[7].

The normal ending of any of these worships consists in the distribution among the faithful, extending it also to mere stand-by, of the already mentioned "Prasada". Such Prasada is what "remains" after the Deities have been presented with the goods and have enjoyed them. Whatever fruit, flower, food or cloths has been offered, is supposed to have reached its Addressees, and been enjoyed by them; this very act of contact has empowered those objects and has rendered them fit to be distributed back to all the presents, beginning with the donors. This Prasada's item is very important in this sort of rites, and it would be worthy a specialized study on the subject, enlarged to include possible similarities in other religions; but, since the character of this work is just to give a gist of the spirit behind Hinduism as a whole, it is enough to have just touched the point and acknowledged its significance and weight.

Though the official Puja requires a regular Pujari entrusted with the care of the consecrated image, private devotions involving presentation of flowers, food, prayers and recitations of devotional verses are open to everybody and very often women can be seen in temples and shrines performing them with all ritualistic paraphernalia of the case. It goes without saying, that in private homes the care of the family Divinities nowadays is mostly in the hands of housewives, except for occasional very pious men or retired senior people.

ii) Murtis

All what has been said up to now regarding Puja evidently requires the presence of the Deities in a tangible form, an image of sort that could be made the receiver of the formal act of worship. In the Vedic period their presence in idols was not required, as it has been stated previously, since it was Agni, on the fireplace in the altar, who took over himself the task of delivering the offerings; but with respect to Puja the position changes.

Puja, in fact, is a devotional action that functions on a different level and mostly, at least in principle, for a different layer of people: the Sudras, the women in general and the not yet initiated children. (Yet, in practice, as already hinted upon, the domain of Puja spread throughout the members of the upper castes as well). The Puja's world and doctrinal background is essentially dualistic, and the devotee, directly or through the intermediary of his pujari, places him or herself in front of a powerful God or Goddess, paying Him or Her homage, offering presents symbolising one's inner reverence and gratefully receiving back the Deity's grace in the form of Prasada.

The Murti, then, make up an iconography that coincide with the literary descriptions found in Epics and Puranas, each God and Goddess singled out with His or Her special attributions. When these attributes are many the Murtis are equipped with as many arms and hands for conveniently holding them all. With the basic Indian tendency to simplification, possibly to counteract the complexity of tropical nature and climate, it is not rare to find one single attribute taken to represent the whole and exhibited in the cult at the place of the full image. Thus, for Puja's sake, it is enough to put a few coins on a metallic plate to symbolise Lakshmi the Goddess of Wealth and Good Fortune; or a Trishula, i.e., a Trident, to represent Shiva, a Discus for Visnu or a Book for Sarasvati, the Goddess of Learning and Arts. We shall discuss these Deities in the next chapter.

The Murtis in general—though there are exceptions to such 'generality'—are fashioned as permanent images and when installed in temples, shrines, and even, sometimes, in the places reserved to them in private houses or huts, are duly consecrated so that the Divine is called upon them in order to be installed in them. From then on, their needs had to be taken care of and regular worship becomes essential. During Festivals such worship is intensified and temples' visits become more frequent. Nevertheless, these are occasions in which not only Temple worship assumes a more elaborated form, but also a special cult is temporary established in a chosen place outside temple premises and temporary Murtis (*utsava murtis*) are prepared and installed after having been properly consecrated. Then they are worshipped with great pomp for the time required by the festivities (in some occasions even up to the last three days of the nine days worship after both the equinox's new moons). At the end of the allotted period, the Murtis are again 'dissacralised', that is 'emptied of the Divine presence', and the images thus devoided of power— but still somehow carrying the imprint of it—are disposed off generally thrown in current waters (where a river is at a reachable distance). Their removal is necessary in order to avoid redundancy; but, apart the possibility of fostering detachment, (These Murtis are ephemeral pieces of art engaging the full skill of their makers and meant to disappear from the mist of human beings after extracting from them the best of their abilities, devotions, times and dedication) their ephemerality can be interpreted also as a kind of overlapping of the Vedic Yajnic spirit bent toward a direct divine-human relationship aiming at inserting a 'monistic' or 'advaitic' goal into the Puja's dualistic mood and doctrine. The Murtis raised for festive occasions enhance for a while the dualistic sense of bowing in front of Something different from one's mortal and limited nature; yet, at the same time, the drastic removal of them remind the worshippers that in the realm of a deeper Reality there is actually nothing radically different from the worshipper himself, nothing that can stand for long as a comfortable counterpart on which to lean for support or to load it with one's problems and difficulties.

On this effect, the Murtis, besides fulfilling the role of concretising the Divine into external, visible forms, so as to appear as the Other Pole of a Duality, can also be 'used' as means for 'trapping' human consciousness when taken as points on which to focus one's attention during meditation. Their actual presence, completed with all their attributes and traditional shapes, serves to capture the concentration of the meditating person when this still needs to be projected outside itself. In this way the Image acts on the visual plan as the sound of a repeated Mantra acts on the auditory level. The hint of a possible disappearance when its role has been fulfilled is an allusion, a clue for the advanced spiritual being that little by little a time will come when no external devise will be required and whatever concept of the Divine shall remain alive in him/her selves would be internalised. For the common devotee, however, that 'departure' of the Murti shall only mean that the special time of festival is over and the 'extra-dose' of Divinity, who came down to reinforce people need of a duality in order to carry on with their difficult lives, is again retiring where it originally belongs.

Some of the Murtis, moreover, especially the ones worshipped at home and installed in occasion of the festivals dedicated to their corresponding Deities—like Lakshmi and Ganesh, for instance, out of Lakshmi Puja in the automn's equinox; or Sarasvati at the entrance of Spring—are kept for the length of the full year after the festivals and then replaced with new Murtis, duly consecrated during the next festivities, while the old images are disposed off into the nearest river. In this replacement enters the idea of a renovation of energy, conforming to the task of rituals, which is to "render new the old" (GopBr) so that the Deities of the house get new bodies properly recharged for another year.

But Murtis (though by far the most common are artefacts of various materials shaped as statues, and in a lesser degree as pictures) are not always confined to unanimated objects. The Gods who do not disdain clay, wood or stone as receptacle for their descent among men, do not object either to dwell temporarily into human forms: in actors, for instance, enacting the roles of Divinities when performing sacred plays. Such actors are not merely impersonating a part, they actually *are* for the time being the God or Goddess that has possessed their bodies when acting mythical plots for people to witness and enjoy. In this respect, the actors become the recipient of Puja in the same manner and at the same title as a living statue. They are, in fact, duly consecrated as statues are and dessacralised at the end of the play or of the seasonal performance. In their quality of Divinity, the actors—generally male children or young boys—are no longer supposed to touch the ground but have to be carried on shoulders by attendants back and from to the stage and to their resting room.

But for the devotees the person who is more apt to impersonate the Godhead—at least for his/her disciples—is a holy monk (or nun) and especially a guru, a spiritual teacher. He/she is supposed to have reached such a degree of inner perfection that there is not longer solution of continuity between the Divine energy at large and what is found in the inner void of his/her heart. In fact, if a "holy person" is charged with the role of a spiritual guide, or guru, whatever his/her inner feeling and personal achievements—he/she may as yet be on his way to attain full perfection—his very role requires from him to act as God for his disciples. In this case the impersonation of Divinity is not temporary but last as long as the guru-disciple relationship last. When the disciple 'comes himself to age' and reaches perfection on his own—that is, he realises that there is no duality involved between himself and his master or between human being and the Godhead—such impersonification is no longer needed in so far as the Divine is no longer perceived as external and different.

To conclude, once more we are faced with the overall Indian tendency of accepting all points of view together, keeping them side by side according to various levels of awareness and spirituality involved, just giving pre-eminence and prominence to those points that suit people position. Thus, monism or rather non-dualism goes together with dualism; philosophical attainment of a deeper unity with the only One without second of the Upanishad alternates itself with the mythological exposition of many Gods and Goddesses engaged in very humanly and worldly tasks, imposing their presence as an alterity vis-à-vis human behaviour and need for worship. In a word, the social framework imprinted on a crowded community filled to the brim with family members, village neighbours, castes solidarity where everything is collectively done and shared, is counterbalanced by the total solitude of the sage and by the walk of individuals on the path of spiritual salvation. The religious coordinates, though devised for the benefit of society and of the collectivist as such, are more often than not open to the personal escape into a higher level where only the inner proficiency of a lonely spiritual struggle can stride. The use of the Murtis in worship is a case in point. Murtis represent the exteriority of the Divine, with a shape to be hold with the senses and a name for the sake of invocation, and are largely made use of in collective worship or at least in worship carried on by family units on the mundane level of duality; they are also put to a certain use by individual seekers when employing the external aspect of a God for the sake of helping concentration or when taken as a worthy receptacle for their unbound religious love. Finally, however, they shall end up by being internalised altogether and be melted in the furnace of that very love leaving in their place only the empty space in the heart "small than a smallest grain of millet and yet larger than the whole universe" as the Upanishad has it. (Ch.Up III,14,3-4)

iii) Mandalas

Linked with this Brahmanic background, but already in a way quite firmly rooted in the 'new' Pauranic World-view, there is another manner to lead to the main Godhead. This is by depicting It (in whatever form devotees like to meditate upon) as the centre of all the Universes. This type of representation stands as it were as a bridge connecting together both the exigencies: the dualistic need to stand apart from the Divine, thus maintaining one's personality, and the 'monistic' urge of overcoming the split between here and there, He and I, this 'natural' world and the 'supernatural' one. This type of image, called *mandala* is drawn as the geometrical figure we have hinted at when presenting the cultural Vedic world as divided into four according to the 3+1 scheme. It could be visually represented as a square holding a circle with its centre, or with a triangle inserted in it. Taking that as a basic feature, many other figures could be drawn taking in account various other sacred numbers, like five, for instance, or six or seven or eight as the cardinal points, or the one thousand petals of the sacred flower: the lotus. All these geometrical figures, inserted in one another, have been taken to represent various aspects of the Divine Universe and have been considered as a kind of pattern showing a way into the 'labyrinth' of other levels in the spiritual realm. Here also the grades of employment of a Mandala are many and vary according to the exigencies of society, if they are taken for a collective purpose, or to the degree of spiritual attainment of individuals when used by them for guide in meditation.

These drawings, sometimes coloured as well, can be made of purely geometrical forms or may contain in the centre and in its most prominent places (in the corners or in the crossing of lines) the figure of special Deities particularly dear to a community or close to the temperament of the seeker. Tantrics, both Hindu and Buddhist, for instance, make a large use of Mandalas, filled with their special Divinities. Even in certain types of sacred dances (as in the case of Kerala's Kathakali) Mandalas are sometimes drawn with coloured flour or sand as ground for the sacred performance. In these cases, the dancers themselves enhance their inner disposition and concentration by dedicating a full day (or more) to the drawing of such mandala as in a geometrical shape or with the image of the Deity in whose honour the dance would be performed; when completed, they worship it and then destroy it by whirlingly dancing over it.[8] On a more mundane plan, sometimes just considered as a manner of decoration for embellishing temples and houses, they are drawn on the floor in occasion of marriages or other ceremonies. In the South of India housewives just outside the front door of their habitations draw a Mandala every morning. Its original meaning was perhaps a hint that by going out or in the dwelling place one has to cross the universe either to reach its centre or to go out of it. Maybe, however, that in many cases the original meaning is not felt any longer and that people continue to draw them just out of tradition or also with a sense of mere decoration to enhance the beauty of the festive occasions.

A curiosity: in a collective work on sacred art round the world, issued some years ago in Italy, one author dealing with Indian traditions presented this popular drawing and illustrates it with the photo of a woman kneeling in front of her house's door while in the process of doing it. Since the material used for such pictures are coloured flour of various grains, the explanation given below the photo was: she does this beautiful drawing (for which she spent at least twenty minutes if no more) in order to "feed the ants"! (Sic!) Perhaps implying a kind of overstressing of Indian kindness toward animal world...without stopping considering that leaving a few grains in a corner will do the job as well without the need to pass a good deal of a housewife's precious time in enhancing the aesthetic sense of the small insects![9]

c. The priests and the poets

Such cultural features, as have been displayed so far, with the great emphasis bestowed on Yajna as the, at least theoretical, action meant to shape Reality according to a definite Order, rigid and flexible at the same time, so as to square an unmanageable tropical Nature into a texture that could make life liveable and diversity woven into a multifarious pattern, needed—as it is not difficult to perceive—a well organized class of people extremely skilled in their task. In fact, only very capable persons could be able to devise such a pattern, to begin with; and then to keep it going for centuries or even for millennia. Such people were the priests deputed to carry on the difficult rites, and the 'poets', or the 'seers', the rishis, who 'translated' the Divine Eternal Sound into the chants and hymns accompanying the offerings. Often, especially at the beginning of their 'history', the two figures coalesced into a single person, responsible for the whole sacred proceeding. Later, however, the complexity of the whole affair required a distribution of duties and the priests, including the reciters of hymns, were raised to the number of 4, plus its square multiplication to allow for assistants, making 16 of them with an optional supervisor. We have seen their number, names and tasks while presenting Vedic religious setting.

According to this settled pattern reached through the intermediary of the priests and poets, the members of their caste, the Brahmans, became involved quite naturally also in the performance of the other form of worship: Puja. However, such cultic performances remained always somewhat of an inferior stage, so much so that the Pujaris in general are looked down as "lower" with respect to the Purohitas. The latter, in fact, continue their tasks through the centuries by performing the proper social rites essential for maintaining man, aware of the changes occurring in his body and life and for keeping order in his relationship with his fellow beings. Brahmans, then, while supplying lower personel to take care of temples, shrines and the rituals to be performed in pilgrimage places, keep their standard especially when they officiate in private homes during festivals, special celebrations, performance of 'sacraments', and also sessions of Sacred Recitations deemed to bring or increase welfare and good fortune to the sponsors—a kind of shift from the laborious performance of a Yajna into its shorter simplification retaining only the power of the sacred utterance, as seen before. In other words, the priestly class continue to maintain for themselves the position of intermediary between ordinary men engaged in worldly tasks and their Gods whom Brahmans represent in their own very persons. Thus, when Yajna was considered definitely superseded at least with respect to the vast majority of religious population, most of the unfulfilled sacred actions turned to worthy substitutes, such as recitation of hymns and religious texts, feeding Brahmans as representatives of the Divine, together with feeding the Ancestors and the human beings in the persons of guests or of the poor.

In principle, Brahmans, being a 'pure' lot because of their dealing with the Purity of the Sacred, could not share food with people belonging to lower castes; their 'duty' then to be fed by others even of the lowest category—because Puja worship was just intended for reaching those people that could not even theoretically enjoying the fruit of 'higher knowledge' as previously seen—created a problem of protocol which was solved by the ritual identification (for the purpose of worship) of the Brahmans with the sacrificial ground in which Agni burns as digestive fire.

In ancient times, when tradition was still in its building, the poets, together with the sacrificing priests, had a deep role to perform in so far as on them fell the task of supplying the sacred Mantras for recitation when such Mantras had to be composed anew. The better the verses and the songs, the higher their power on the Gods and the stronger their own inner energy. In the Rigveda there are hints to this effect as seen before. But already at the time of the wholly reshaping of Brahmanic culture when Yajurveda was composed together with the Brahmanas, the tendency is to confine recitation to the hymns of the far back inheritance, till those hymns, divided in the respective branches suiting sacrificial order and distributed to the specific assignments of the various priests, as specified in a previous chapter, became the fixed patrimony of Vedic lore. The task of the reciting priests, from then on, was that of repeating those hymns and verses—*in toto aut in partes*—to perfection without introducing the slightest change or modification. When, however, the different type of sacred literature, epic and pauranic, began to be widely spread to the point of practically taking over the role of the Vedas as the Fifth One, the first reciters were still allowed to add to the lot according to their inspiration, interpretation and adaptation to personal situations, social contexts, religious needs of the times; till even these contributions little by little ceased to be innovative and adaptation to worldly changes were restrained to comments and pertinent explanations.

This stress of the preponderant role played by human beings, even if specialised human beings, in shaping the religious and cultural world would, perhaps, surprise readers of different cultures—especially Westerners—or would give them the wrong feeling that the exposer of these notes—a Westerner herself—has been yielding a bit too much to positivistic theories for which what religion consider to be "revelations" directly from the Divinity is but the unavoidable "working up" of clever self-styled 'holders' of such so called 'revelations'. However, this is precisely the outstanding feature that runs along the whole bulk of Brahmanic-Hindu religion right from earliest times down to present day situation. Though some of the philosophical classical schools have argued and demonstrated that the Vedas were *aparusheya*, without (human) Authors, and its Seers did only transmit what they had heard (sruti) of the Eternal Sound, nevertheless all along the various texts there is a constant reference to the creative role of the poets, (the Vedic as well as the Epic and Pauranic ones) even in shaping and handing over to common people the ways Gods and Goddesses are and behave. It even looks like that the whole cultural and religious construction is but a product of human mind— a proposal to which many atheists would gladly subscribe. The point, however, is that Indian poets and priests, together with philosophers and spiritual teachers (gurus), are not atheists and never were. But Indians are, in spite of what is normally believed by some Westerner positivists, very rational and concrete thinkers. To all effects, whatever men know about the Divine comes to them through the mediation of special human beings; they have experienced in the inner recesses of their selves the power of an 'otherworldly' Energy which has swallowed them up and which they subsequently, for the rest of their lives, endeavour to translate into comprehensible images that could be understood by the others. That 'privilege' of being directly connected with that Impersonal Force, beyond words and even concepts for those perceiving it, is theoretically opens to all, but in practice it is the prerogative of extremely few persons, and in all respects are they who become the responsible of whatever form 'revelation' would be disclosed. This situation is true, as all the 'atheist' scholars would subscribe, for all religions of the world, only that everywhere, except in India, the Divine Authority is named as the sole and unique source of whatever religion stands for. In India such drastic division between the Divine and the human, the Source and the receivers of the Divine message, is not so important because there is no risk that even the common people would belittle the role and the position of the Divine. On the contrary, they bestow a divinised role to their Rishis and 'realised' spiritual persons; people officially recognise the latter as being One and the same thing with the Absolute they endeavour to describe and their awareness of the "ways of the Spirit" is deemed to be such that the poets are supposed to impart their knowledge and intuitions also to the Deities themselves. We shall quote later on, when dealing directly with the Divine and the Divinities in the next chapter, a Pauranic text in which a break of the Impersonal Absolute occurs among the Gods gathered in Krishna's Heaven; the havoc this sudden irruption causes to the upset Deities is clarified and explained to them by the heavenly poet Narada (BrVaivPur). It is true that, already in the Brahmanas, this situation is somehow restored to its balance by the divinisation of the Seven main Rishis authors of the ancient hymns, who, being the creators of the basic principles of their entire culture, have being extolled as Divine and elevated to the highest possible rang as Creators of the Universe, so that a kind of line could be drawn again between the human specimen of this Earth and the Heavenly or Divine dimension; however the Seven Rishis are also related to this very world by their 'direct' descendents—the human families connected with each of them in their respective Gotras (roughly the equivalent of the Latin Gentes)—and, most important, the same position of highest spiritual authority recognised to 'realised' persons continue to be valid up to our own times, thus giving us the opportunity to witness the process and procedures of antiquity and to ascertain the validity of the creative role assigned to the founders and builders of Vedic and Hindu world-views.

d. Pilgrimages (*Tirthayatra*)

To keep in tune with our fourfold mandalic division we will concern ourselves here with pilgrimages. This type of Hindu devotion is properly attached to Pauranic mentality and deals with the importance bestowed on special places supposedly to be connected with one or another Deity or with some particularly powerful or sacred areas. Obviously, this kind of attraction for a fixed spot can hardly be seen as a heritage from the nomadic far away past—as it is the case of most rites and customs connected with Vedic and Brahmanic visions—with all the wealth of hidden and forgotten memories of a mythical lost perfection (as often the case with other religions and also with the cherished preservation of obsolete gestures or customs just because they remind of a long lost 'perfect situation'). In that nomadic past everything was perpetually on the move and we have seen how the Yajnic worship still retains the flavour of that situation by being performed on a temporary settlement built for the purpose and totally destroyed at the end of it. Yet, with the transference of the high conception of an Impersonal All-comprehending Divine into well shaped and constructed mythical Divine figures, with Murti as tangible representations, temples and shrines for dwelling places, and special locations attached to their myths or stories, such locations raised high in the esteem of devotees and became, quite naturally, destination of pilgrimages.

Yet, one may be justified to ask oneself whether really there is no inner connection between the Yajna-form of worship on one side, and the Pilgrimage urge of the Pauranic mentality on the other. Generally, in spite external appearances, Indian thought does not proceed by vast unconnected jump from one vision to another. There is always a kind of link, subtle derivation, that makes the passage smooth and above all allows easy shifts to and fro from the 'old background' to the 'new' take over. Where, then, pilgrimage could stand with respect to the basic relevant Past? Can a link be detected between the never fixed main ritualistic Vedic performance and the common practice of Hindu predilection for pilgrimage's places and the timing attached to them? The answer can come in the form of a Myth, or a Pauranic Katha. Once upon a time...a king, decided to perform a solemn sacrifice, but though his own daughter Sati was formally married to the God Shiva (of whom we shall speak in the coming chapter), his son-in-law was not invited because of the roughness of His ascetic manners. In the mist of the performance, however, the excluded Deity busted in a whirl of righteous fury and, willingly and in full awareness, polluted the whole place. But He claimed with violence his due portion (*bhaga*) before destroying everything. He is, somehow, depicted, as it seems, as the enemy and destroyer of the old way of worship in favour of a different path of approaching Divinity; nevertheless He resented the exclusion and exacted his sharing in the offerings (the Bhaga that came to designate his holder as Bhagavan, the Supreme Lord as the Powerful through Bhaga) as essential to his very position. So, the destroyer but also the preserver, because asserter of his stolen divine rights.

But the story continues by reporting that his wife, covered with shame for the default of her own father, threw herself into the still burning sacred fire, as an offering and as an atonement. Shiva, the love full spouse, became literally mad with sorrow and grabbing the corpse of his wife started off into a maddening dance whirling around all over the country in sheer despair, till the other great God of Pauranic mythology: Vishnu, had to intervene and stop the maddening dance, by making the body of the

Goddess falling down into pieces all over the places: a hand or arm here, a leg there, her earring on still another spot (in the centre of the holy city of Benares). Later, Sati was restored to him as Uma in a new rebirth. The places blessed with those pieces became the most important sites of pilgrimage especially in North and Middle India. Thus the link was established between one ritual practice with the other and this through the active mediation of one of the two main Godheads at the top of their respective Pantheons.(42) We shall come back to Him at the proper place, where we shall also attempt to find out His position with respect to the main traditional creative worship, Yajna.

Pilgrimage places fall into various categories. There are some, like Benares for instance, whose sacrality is a permanent beckoning open to pilgrims all time round the year, only with a natural inclination to reach the spot during special festivities or specific occasions like for instance, an inauspicious eclipse. Others have naturally fallen into a seasonal periodicity, having to observe the viability of the roads leading there; this applies especially to mountains temples or Gods' epiphanies in some high peaks whose paths are closed due to snow falls and life on the spot extremely harsh and almost endurable. Others, still—and this is valid especially for the four main sites near rivers or a lake from East, North and West India: Allahabad or Prayag, Hardwar, Ujjain and Nasik respectively, connected with the Shiva's story—are arranged to take place during specific astronomic conjunctions every 12 years in each city, which means that such holy pilgrimages are open every three years for people to assemble. In these sacred places, as in the other pilgrimage's spots, prescribed rites are to be performed by the devotees culminating with a ritual bath in the river. But the speciality of these gathering is that the event attracts on the spot a great number of sadhus, gurus, holy people...in a word the main masters of spirituality and religious traditions giving them the opportunity of seizing the occasion for meeting together, exchange points of view, discussing spiritual attainments, publicising them...In short, from this perspective pilgrimages of this kind take the place of the ancient Yajnas where the respective sponsors afforded to extend their hospitality to a large number of spiritual masters, wandering monks, priests and philosophers, that is, the cream of the people responsible for the creation, maintenance and transmission of the main traditional tenets, giving them the possibility of exchanging views and clarifying doubts or sharing knowledge. When the occasions for such gathering became so few as to become practically inexistent, pilgrimages conveniently spaced out took over the Vedic task to provide chances for learned spiritual discussions among the main responsible of keeping tradition not only alive but also vibrant of vitality, thus offering the opportunity for assuring the essential unity to the background of personal and regional Diversity[10].

We are again faced here with the principle of "nothing is lost, nothing is destroyed, but everything is changing and transforming itself", though still continuing to remain intact when suitable occasions allow it to come to the surface.

We have said, previously, that in India there are certain prevailing conditions, both climatic and geographical, for which the passage of time does not leave marks yielding to a linear sequence of events or of "'epochal' moods". Here the above quoted dictum: "Nothing is created and nothing destroyed, but every thing is transformed"...is wonderfully put into practice. Transformed, yes, but also persistent, kept unchanged through the millennia like for instance the Vedic layer of Yajnic practices image of Divinities, still never died or sank too low in the background as to be forgotten. Yajna— or at least some forms of it in an adapted way—is still performed occasionally, while the cultural world-view depending on it represents still, as seen, the back-bone and even the full skeleton of social foundations and assumptions and of its spiritual conquests. And this is due, essentially, to Indian orthodox Brahmans and to the high role shouldered by the Gurus. The Gurus, when belonging to the devotional schools, are considered to be—and mostly they are, through their personal achievements—directly linked to the Divinity of their love, so that they can be righteously reckoned as their mouthpiece or 'microphone'. If the Gurus belong to the non-dualistic schools of knowledge (see it discussed in IV. B.), then their position is theoretically even stronger: they, being directly identified with that Absolute Power, are in the position to deliver the spiritual and socio-religious message as if on first person. They can explain, adapt, interpreter, present and even occasionally change, the main traditional issues; they have the authority to do it and, though the Vedic and even Epic bulk is definitely close to manipulation, their contributions enter in the tradition as such. See for instance how the stands taken by persons like Ramana Maharshi or Anandamayi Ma tend to become canonical not only among their respective disciples.

These modern examples can provide the key notes for playing the religious motives openly elaborated by human figures, and therefore to understand why there is no need for Hindus to minimise the creative role performed by men lest they should become conceited, or their 'this-worldly' personality would obliterate the necessity of a 'transcendent' Personal

Divinity or Impersonal Divine—according to the various ways of reacting to such 'Heavenly' Power—the fact is that there is not division between the two. No every man, in fact, is entitled to 'speak in behalf of the Divine' or to transmit with authority the leading principles of a whole culture, but only those who have worked themselves spiritually to such an extent as to totally obliterating themselves as separated personalities—not only the 'non-dualistic' seers, but also the dualistic devotees of a given Deity: they also have to if not ontologically disappear as separate identities at least to wipe away from them any remaining consciousness of themselves. Only them and only then—that is, when reached such a status—they can "play the tune" and their "play" is tantamount for Divine "revelation". But a Revelation that is never seen as definitive and also that is never taken so seriously that fun cannot be made about. After all are also human beings the persons involved with this all, and, as we shall see a little further, their presentation of Divine figures is always slightly (sometimes not even that lightly) tinged with a sense of humour.

NOTES

1. See P V Kane, *History of Dharma Shashtra*, 5 vols. *Op cit*
2. Though an inverted datation because historically the Ramayana ranges earlier than the Mahabharata
3. See a popular summary by C Rajagopalachari published by Bharatia Vidya Bhavan Mumbai 1951
4. See a popular summary by C Rajagopalachari published by Bharatia Vidya Bhavan Mumbai 1951
5. See e.g. Bhagavata Purana, Brahmavaiavarta P etc.
6. Their figures are said to be raised in the minds of Vyasa and Valmiki
7. I witnessed such a powerful outburst in Chidamabaram (1963)
8. I witnessed this in a Keralite dance in New Delhi under the patronage of IGNCA in 1986, and another longer week long drawing of such a mandala by Tibetan Monks in Rome, immediately thrown into the Tiber a day after its completion
9. Do not think it idle to have pointed out this little flaw in a book meant for a large public. It shows that there is still some readiness to 'play the fool' with people whose culture and way of understanding Nature and Reality is different from one's own.
10. Just to name a few: Badrinath connected with Vishnu, and Kedarnath with Shiva; in the Himalaya Uttar Kashi and Gangotri as the sources of the sacred River Ganga together with Rishikesh and Haridwar where this river reaches the plains; and the places connected with sacred rivers like the Ganga her sister Jamuna and the Kaveri in the South etc. a special position is given to mount Kailasha together with the nearby lake Mansarovar as the dwelling place of the gods as Olympus in Greece. See B N Saraswati, tradition f tirthas in India, Varanasi (N K Bose Memorial foundation) 1983.

CHAPTER 3
The Divine And The Deities

A nd now, after having mentioned the Divine in Its absoluteness as well as in its different visible forms, it is time to tackle It directly. According to what has been said up to this moment, during the very long period of Vedic-Hindu religion—covering several millennia—several layers of various ways to conceive and represent Divinities and their Divine unique Source have been noticed. And since, as mentioned all along, "nothing is really destroyed or discarded, as nothing is really completely born anew" all these layers are variously permeated in several degrees, while at the same time maintaining a rather well defined distinction among themselves and their respective characteristics.

a. The Vedic Pantheon and its Impersonal Source

The first of these layers is, obviously, represented by the Divinities praised by the Rgvedic and Atharvavedic Hymns, when considered in their *vaikhari* aspect (that is its overt level of plain communication)[1]. It consists in many Deities (mostly males with Usha, the Dawn, as an important main Goddess) bearing in names and characters a strong similarity with the Pantheon-s worshiped by the other Indo-European tribes who in several waves beginning from or before c. 2000 B.C. onwards migrated toward the West. All of them venerated a Sky-God, master of Thunderbolt, who has been preceded by a superseded Primordial Couple of Great Gods: a Sky Father and Earth Mother and a High God (ex.), with or without his female counterpart; a Messenger of the Gods; the Twin Divinities identified with the two main stars of the constellation Gemini, by all mentioned as "Herald to the Sun" (an attribute that could be taken as a good point for dating at least the period when this worship started: Gemini heralded the Sun in Spring Equinox when the latter was in Cancer, a feature happening between c 8000-6000); a God of different weight in the various Indo-

European cultures symbolised by the Sun and one by the Moon; a Divinity presiding over the particularly important element of Fire, and so on.[2]

The Vedic main God, holder of the Thunderbolt, is Indra (sometimes titled also Brihaspati—the Lord of Speech), the strong male warrior who lead the various kings at the head of the moving tribes into victory over rivals of the same racial stock and in their sweeping down into new grounds, therefore facing the local Protectors as bad Spirits or Demons (the Rakshasas, and others that had to be kept away from the Aryans pure sacrificial grounds). He was, therefore, the obvious Deity and Defender of the Kshatriya class, the fighting warriors of a victorious people. Indra, in his turn, was somehow preceded by Varuna, who, however, is quite an active Deity in his own right, alone or coupled with the bright (solar) God Mitra, the Friend. The Asvins, or Gemini stars, are also the receivers of several hymns and their exploits often hinted upon as 'known stuff' that needed only a short reminder for bringing back to memory the whole issue. The trouble with this 'obviousness' became a veritable impasse when, a good many centuries later, these feats alluded upon were totally forgotten and had to be guessed again or even totally built up anew. However, the main important God was and is Agni, the (sacrificial) Fire, the main Divinity of the officiating Brahmans, the Mediator between the worshipers and the Worshiped Gods, a Protector and Defender of his people able to stir His supernatural heat into a strong ritually striking weapon. And since this weapon can be most dangerously used against rivals of the same 'race' using the same rites and the same Sacrificial Fire, it becomes imperative not only to gain His favours but also to divert it from the rivals. Agni, as the main Sacrificial God, is also somewhat connected with creation and with the maintenance of such creation, and to this day his prestige has not faded away—to the contrary that of Indra who with time and the change of cultural mood stepped down to a secondary position or rank, his past greatness remaining mainly in the 'onomatology'. Furthermore, in the Rigvedic Hymns there is repeated mention of compound Deities, like Indra-Varuna, Mitra-Varuna, Indragni, and one gets the impression, all along the display of the hymns in their respective family-mandalas or Books, that we are left with the cream of ancient rishis cultic praises, each preferably extolling his protective favourite God[3]. On this basis one can even try to unearth the later family-feud between the Vasistas and the Visvamitras, a feud started as far as their heads were concerned, ending in the Rigveda itself with the temporary victory of the latter just to be overthrown in his turn by the descendants of his rival, who, in the Pauranic legends degraded Visvamitra to the rank of a king struggling to acquire (or to conquer again?) his Brahmanic position[4]. One can deduce this by analysing the main thread of their quarrel in the few hints recorded in the hymns of their respective Books (the III for the Visvamitras, the VII for the Vasisthas) and also by considering the strong position hold by Agni as main Deity in the so called 'kshatriya' rishi against Indra and Indravaruna invoked by the Brahman par excellence[5].

Many other Gods and Goddesses mentioned in the first and last Vedas, the two that betray traces of a most ancient situation and way of life, seem to a superficial consideration to be embodiment of natural phenomena and elements, like Sun, Moon, some stars, Wind, Fire, Rain, Storms, and the like, so much so that the old school of the first Western scholars dealing with such religious matter had no qualms in defining them all as "Naturistic Divinities". Actually, though those connections could not be denied, a Deity is always infinitely deeper, ampler and meaningful than the mere phenomenon they recall through their names or epithets. For each of these Gods and Goddesses, so full of significance in cultic and cultural depth, a few descriptive lines can never do proper justice to them, they all deserving full monographs for themselves—monographs that, by the way, have been provided for many of them since decades from the past century onward. We, therefore, would not linger on them any'longer and shift our attention to their 'inner' development.

It is difficult at this point to try to pin down a development or a slow inner transformation of the whole "*materia divina*". In the hymns themselves there are several layers by now so welded together that is nearly impossible to give them a linear exposition. Their features, after all, is preserved in the Sacred Literature, which, as seen, carries within itself the mark of several 'editing', the most important of which was that impressed to the whole material by its last Vyasa during their main session at Kurukshetra and Naimisharanya. Here, the rishis, though putting into a proper order the main tenets of a very ancient patrimony that they passed over as they were, had nevertheless already reached the inner awareness of the main underlining unity of all the divine figures addressed in the hymns. This deep 'philosophical' or 'mystical' truth emerges in many hymns of the last Book or Mandala (as they are usually called, probably without reference to the drawn ones) added as first and last of the just forming up Corpus. There we are even faced with attempts to overcome multiplicity in divine figures into the idea of a deeper unity beyond them all (RV I.164.49; cfr RV III.55). There also appears the figure of the Great Man, the Maha Purusha, as a Cosmic image connected with Sacrifice, with Yajna, as the main Victim immolated by the Gods who 'saw' the creative power released in the act of his ritual cutting into "Portions", or of his dismemberment. (RV I.164.1.ff and X.90.1ff). Side by side to it, or in a following sequence of meditations concerning the main Sacrificial Action, the Rishis had the intuition of an all-encompassing, yet full transcendent, impersonal Entity—*sat*—yawning beyond and behind the various religious forms praised and worshiped in the hymns themselves. Is it the first perception of the Void peering out through the vastness of the planes they had just come to settle in? There are a few hymns in the Xth Mandala that are unsurpassed for their breath taking glances into such Impersonal Infinity, into the One or even above and previous to the One:

"At the beginning neither Sat nor A-sat was there...then the One emerged through the power of his own Heat..." (RV. X.129.1&3)

What seems to have lead to this more profound description of an inner experience, which normally defies ordinary human expressions, is a kind of dissatisfaction with the usual concept of the Deities to whom sacrifice was offered. After Sacrifice itself has grown under the speculative drive of the priests, busy to publicising it on one hand and to dig into its depths in order to discover layers upon layers of hidden significance into it, on the other, the former Addressees paled before the growth of the Action as such. They became dependent on It and, in order to avoid being dependent on the whimsical decision of men to offer them at all—one has to keep in mind that Vedic Yajnas were occasional and not periodical—transferred their position from Receivers to Performers.[6] There was, then, the need to look for something more adequate to cope with a cult that, though drawing its power mainly through doctrine and theory, had been incremented to such an extent as to become the focal point of the whole Universe. Thus the query of the rishis when, puzzled by the magnitude of their findings, turned perplexed with offerings in their hands to look for a more adequate Recipient:

"To whom (kasmai) shall we give the offering?" (RV X.121 refrain)

The answer perhaps was not given and what is found at the end of the hymn: "To Prajapati" the Lord of creatures, the main Godhead of the Brahmanas, could be a later interpolation.

b. The Brahmanic Divinity and Its children: Devas and Asuras

When, in fact, Sacrifice grew under their very hands into the Cosmic creative Action par excellence, through the divinisation of the offering (as I have already shown in another book)[7], that offering, embodied in its higher victim (which should have been the Horse, but for the purpose of its divinisation was identified with the figure of the Cosmic Man, the Purusha) concretised Itself into the main Godhead, Victim as well as Its Immolator and Its Receiver. The whole Action expanded and closed within its own unique identity, the entire creation becoming as the systole and diastole (say, the higher and lower limits of the heart pulsations) of a single procedure and so begetting the idea of a Single God bursting Himself from within into the multiplicity of creation, either as the product of his own Self-immolation and consequent dismemberment, or, as later envisaged in a different image, by splitting himself into two (his two male and female parts) driven at it by a sudden awareness of his solitude; a solitude that was first perceived as fear and then as boredom. (BrArUp I,4,1ff)

As it appears, then, the huge task of adapting their culture to a new and different environment altogether, coupled with the drastic change into a sedentary life and activity, was so deep and involving that practically it can be said that a new concept of the Divine itself grew up straight from the rishis meditations on their main sacred cultic action. I have elsewhere already sketched the process concerned using the following images...

type 1: $\alpha\text{-}S\text{-}\Omega$: type 2: $\alpha\text{-}\widehat{S}\text{-}\Omega$

...where the usual scheme, represented by type 1 in which the human offering shoots up to the Gods and reaps its reward in the reverse direction, is transformed into type 2 in which the offering itself become the focus of the whole Action overflowing with its abundance into both the world of Gods and that of men in equal measure. That 'Victim', thus, became automatically divinised and is found in the Brahmanic texts as the Supreme Godhead, the Father of all creatures born from His sacrificial dismemberment and existing alone before even the beginning of Time. He is Prajapati, the Lord of Creatures[8]. His first emitted Son is Agni, as seen when the Agnicayana rite was described, and then all his other children were born. They soon divided themselves into two groups: the first-born Asuras, representing the evil side of creation through their ill use of sacrifice as such, and the Devas, lead by their chief Indra of Vedic memory, representing Goodness and soon contending with their elder rivals in an endless strife to secure for themselves the benefits deriving from a good mastering of 'Yajnic' rites. Most of the Brahmanic stories dealing with aetiological topics refer to such a rivalry as the main starting point.

In this resettling of mythology, cosmology and cosmogonies found in the Brahmanas, the ancient Vedic Gods, the Devas, have sung into an amorphous nameless group, headed by their earlier chief Indra, thus being stripped of their distinct personalities—but for the few exceptions—and becoming rather equalised with their elder brothers, the Asuras, also essentially an homogeneous nameless group. The only outstanding personalities of the two parties are their respective Gurus, called Brhaspati (the Lord of Speech) and Sukra, identified respectively with the planets Juppiter (Brihaspati in Sanskrit) and Venus (Sukra in Sanscrit) who entertain with one another a friendly relationship as collegues. Escaping such uniformity is, obviously, Agni and besides also Usha the Dawn, Indra the chieftain, the Asvins the healers, and occasionally someone else according to local needs or preference. In their falling into anonymousness, furthermore, they lost somehow also their power, because, more often then not, in the cosmogonic conflicts staged with their brothers-rivals, they are invariably defeated, only to be rescued in a second time through a better understanding and a more correct performance of the right rituals[9].

As it can be seen, this overpowering position assumed by Brahmanic essentially theoretical Sacrificial rites had not only the effect of lessening the figures of the ancient Gods, but also that of inserting a certain degree of weakness or even blame in their own conduct. And such blame had the tendency to grow into 'something' that can attain also the Absolute or at least the main sacrificial Godhead. In fact, if the conduct of the Devas and Asuras are sometimes reproachable—the Asuras as their permanent feature, not only because born as shadows from Prajapati, but also as brought about by their ill management of rites; the Devas by their newly developed constant early defeat to their rivals—also Prajapati's behaviour is not always blemishless. Apart the fact that Prajapati, as the only Creator, is responsible for the entrance in the worlds of such evils as Hunger and Death, besides the presence of the Asuras as shadows and opponents, his very sons, the Devas, strongly objected to one of his ways of creating living species by pursuing and copulating with his own daughter Usha, their sister. The righteously angry Gods turned against their Father and as a punishment submitted him to the same treatment (castration) applied to the overthrown Supreme God in Greek as well as Roman mythologies. Is this act a manner to signify that creation in its active form is over and the Creator responsible for it has to be emasculated in order to stop dangerous excess? Or is it a way for the weakened traditional Gods to try to get again some of the ancient power by depriving of it the Supreme Entity? In a different myth or story Indra boldly requests his Father to entrust him with Sovereignty over the Devas by transfers again to Him the power of creation; then, to the bewildered Godhead asking: "but if I gave it to you, who shall I be?" He answers: "just what you said: Who? This shall be your name, the name you can be invoked with in cult"[10]. And when philosophers have reached such an attribute for their main God, this one looks very much as if he is on his way to vanish from the cultic horizon[11].

But this, somehow, is also the fate, which seems to be awaiting the Brahmanic Sacrifice itself. Not that it ever get wiped out altogether—the Epics and Historic texts, *Itihasas*, still report of such ceremonies performed by great kings at the peak of their power and glory—but it lost its overwhelming importance in the moulding of cultural background and coordinates. New cultic exigencies, as we have already seen, were stepping forwards in order to include in their celebrations other layers of population; and with these new forms of worship coming to the front also the Deities receiving it were growing into new shapes and personalities. And here we reach another of the peculiarities of this fluid and yet static religion that Brahmanism is. Though, as it seems, the main effort of setting down religious, spiritual and cultural coordinates has been beared by the rishis and thinkers of the Brahmanic times (corresponding to the period represented by the Brahmana and Sutra texts)[12] the conception of the Divine connected with their vision of Yajna looks somewhat like a kind of transition between the Vedic Gods inherited by the Past through the hymns employed in the theorical cult, and the Gods getting the upper hand in the rising popular religion and worship. However, this may also be a feeling brought about by modern scholarship, with its tendency to glide over the literature represented by the Brahmanas as too 'ritualistic' therefore boring and obsolete, successfully backed by ordinary Hindu devotees, for whom, if Vedas and Upanishads still hold a faint echo in their minds, the Brahmanas have almost totally faded away from their awareness[13]. Actually, Prajapati is still a mentioned entity and the eternal struggle between evil and goodness, light and darkness, positive and negative realities (proper to human experience and alive in all traditions of the world) is still looked upon in terms of the Devas and Asuras opposition, side by side the more dynamic battle between a given 'Hindu' God or Goddess and his or her Demonic antagonist.

c. The Epic and Pauranic Deities: Vishnu and Shiva

It has been seen, when dealing with the Sacred Literature, that the 'rising of Hinduism' was essentially an answer to the necessity of getting the non-initiated ones participate in the Knowledge of the Divine. The philosophical Truth presented in the Vedas and further deepened by the meditation and elaboration of Brahmanic sages had reached, both in its ritual-

istic aspect and in its spiritual profundity, a degree of such a sophistica-
tion as to become not only incomprehensible to the majority of people, but
also dangerous to enter in contact with for ordinary persons. Its tradition
could only remain alive within the restricted circle of the Brahmins left in
charge of the preservation of this ancient literature, thus sinking in the
background and becoming an esoteric reality for the 'apotropaic' use of
the few.

As for the greater portion of humanity, such Truth needed to acquire
an understandable shape and a graspable meaning; and this could be
obtained by presenting it in the form of Personal Deities. These, then, for
the very fact of 'revealing' themselves in such a fashion, had to show
themselves with a definite and visible aspect, representable in a given
iconography—as previously discussed—and equipped with definite
personalities and stories (*katha* or myths) outlining their character and
activities.

Since the resulting Divine figures are but personification of the deep
Vedic wisdom about Supreme Reality and Its relationship with the
phenomenic worlds in their coming to be, preservation and final
reabsorption, these three features became the main cores and outstanding
points of reference for the activities of the ensuing Deities. These features
became even the distinguishing characteristics by which the main Divinities
are known through the ages as the Creator, the Preserver and the Destroyer
side by side with their 'proper' names: Brahma, Vishnu and Shiva. Actually,
however, the 'popular' religion of India, since the beginning of its emerging
shape, has grown in two main groups or branches (not sects as normally
referred to because "sect" and "sectarianism" imply from their start a
"cutting", a "division" from a main organism like Protestant Sects with
respect to Christian Catholicism) each headed by one of the two main
Supreme Gods: Vishnu and Shiva. Such Gods held the central position in
their own respective Pantheons and are responsible for the three stages of
the 'created worlds' or worldly Reality. Each of them did it, according to
their respective mythologies, in his own way and assisted by his own
helpers or counterpart: Brahma in the case of Vishnu; the Feminine Principle,
the Shakti, in the case of Shiva. And while Brahma, the first God of the
commonly known Trimurti, gradually lost his independence till almost
disappearing from worship, on the contrary the originally Shivaitic Shakti
in certain geographical areas (like Bengal and the Mountains) had her cult
so developed that she almost became an independent Entity by herself,
leading an independent group[14].

i) Vishnu

Since what is called 'Hinduism' is but a more understandable expression of Vedic wisdom, it is obvious that the name of at least the highest Divinities should be traced in the ancient sacred hymns and literature. This is specially to be expected for the Supreme God of the branch which seems more directly involved with the presentation—and, later on, continuation—of the religious feeling and cultural setting brought about by Yajna's theory: i.e. Vishnu. In the Rigvedic hymns Vishnu is mentioned but seldom and is of secondary importance;(2) nevertheless, in the Brahmanas (see: SatBr VI,1,1,1,) there is a myth that seems to stand for a legitimating to the transfer of power to such a God. Vishnu wins a contest among the other gods for attaining the essence of Yajna. It is true that he had to release it to Indra in a second moment—even loosing his head in the process, head which flew in the sky and became the sun—yet, at any rate, his victory gave him a permanent identification with the ritual power and mentality developed around Brahmanic Sacrifice[15].

Vishnu, in fact, is the head of that religious group that remained traditionally bound to 'ritual purity' and to a mystico-philosophical wisdom and knowledge of the learned spirituality of the past[16]. He is the God of Light, connected with the Sun, the clarity of the Day and the task of creating and maintaining the Universe. In a certain sense one can say that He embodies, better than his counterpart of the other group, the more genuine spirit of 'Brahmanic' mentality. However, He does not create through a ritual action, but essentially from his own inner power stirred up by heat and movement when He wakes up from a long sleep after a Mahayuga of rest. Actually, He does not act directly in creation; He does it through the work of Brahma issued from the Lotus grown from his button-belly on his waking to a new Day, to a new Yuga, inside a given Mahayuga. He also becomes the final Destroyer of such a creation when, after the full cycle of eras have elapsed, He allows his (lower) collaborator Shiva to burn it with cosmic fire before He himself will get loose the cosmic waters on which He would recline to sleep again, over the coils of the cosmic Serpent Sesha, at the completion of another Yuga. In this myth, not only the learned and elaborated conception of Time is made simple and understandable, but the whole process is also put under the activities and patronage of the main Deity, thus giving it the security of a living relationship and of a sympathetic personal concern over possible rising troubles.

Moreover, as representative of the traditional religious trend, Vishnu is made to embody both the innate tendency to plurality proper to an essentially polytheistic mentality as handed down from the far Vedic past, and the philosophical and mystical discovery of an underlying Unity of the highest spiritual Power. To comply with the latter, He is seen and described as the Absolute Godhead, responsible through his Maya—his 'conjurer's power' one could say—for the appearance as well as disappearance of these worlds, but finally the only Existent, One without second, on whose blossom any sage and mystic earns to be (re)absorbed. As far as the former is concerned, Vishnu meets the need of variety manifested by Indian people, exposed, as it has been seen at the beginning, to the multifarious geographical and climatic diversities of the subcontinent, by "descending" to them in various forms and personalities. These "descends", called in Sanskrit *avataras*, are traditionally arranged in the round number of 10—though there is also mention of 24 of them—by the Puranas, but sometimes their lists do not fully agree over their identity. Such descends or "incarnations" (as often are translated in modern languages) are not homogeneous and do not entail the same degree of popularity and worship. Actually the most important of them are two and both are the heroes of the main Indian Epics. One may fairly say that both of them channel the real worship due to Vishnu and that they draw the affection of the devotees with more passion and abandon than a distant Supreme God could arouse. However, their advent is preceded by a series of six previous Avataras, each triggered by the necessity of getting rid of some cosmic or personal evil. Each of these events and figures has its own story and his own inner meaning; nevertheless, seen them from an external point of view (namely, from a rather 'scientific' attitude), they bear a strange connection with the "evolution theory" and they seem to depict the Nature's struggle to mould and reach at a human perfection. They are as follows:

1. Matsya, the Fish. In the proper explanatory myth of the Purana of this name, Vishnu takes this form in order to rescue Manu, the first Lawyer, from the Deluge. Needless to say that this aquatic form of life may also stand to symbolise the emergence of living beings and the role played by Water in their birth and growth.

2. Kurma, the Turtle. As in many mythologies of the world, in this form Vishnu provides a firm support for the foundation of the Earth[17]. This cosmogony role is one of the most widespread ideas among the most different people and religions and found its ritualistic (by now esoteric) counterpart in the turtle incorporated in the first layer of the Agnicayana in a Vedic Soma sacrifice.

3. Varaha, the Boar or wild-pig. This is the form that, already in the Brahmanas (SatBr II 1 1 10ff) Prajapati takes in order to dive on the bottom of the Ocean to fetch some earth with which fashioning the earth[18]. The presence of the Boar in this connection is quite interesting and somewhat intriguing in so far as in many mythologies all over the world this animal bears a strange connection with sacrifice, not only as a victim but also in its concept, and Vishnu, as seen before, has conquered a special identification with the Vedic Yajna. It may also represent the fertility of the Earth and Her depths.

4. Nara-Singha, the Man-lion. Vishnu appears in this form just for rescuing a young devotee from the snares of Evil.[19] In this escalation toward perfection in life, may it not be seen as an attempt of Humanity to free itself from the power of matter and from the animalist governing its body?

5. Vamana, the Dwarf. The myth of this manifestation or descent seems to be an attempt to explain a somewhat cryptic ritual performed by the Yajamana during a sacrificial session: three steps for the conquest of the three worlds (the lower, middle and above)[20]. The story narrates that Vishnu took this form for deceiving a king into granting him as much land as he could cover with three steps, then, becoming a giant covered the universe with the first two and pushed the king in the netherworld with the third. A part that a dwarf becoming a giant is a common feature in Indo-European lore, a dwarf may also be seen as an imperfect human being struggling toward a proper balance, exactly like its counterpart, the overgrown next step.

6. Parashurama, the giant man. He was a skilled Brahmin, master of martial arts who for some reasons hated *kshatriyas* and had to be tricked by one of the epic Heroes into releasing his secret knowledge. On the scale of perfection could not his position after the Dwarf be seen as the excess to be avoided in order to strike the proper equilibrium and harmony? Which is exactly what the 7th incarnation stands for.

7. Rama, the hero of the Ramayana, later converted into a properly worshiped Divine manifestation[21].

8. Krishna or, in other Pauranic lists, his half-brother Balarama. Here too we are on the realm of the Divine as such. If Vishnu's incarnation has to be seen in Balarama, then He Himself came down to destroy Evil by his direct presence in the figure of Krishna; if this 8th Avatara is Krishna himself, then he can be seen as an overflowing of His Divine Power so as to allow a wider and better interaction with his devotees in a transport of mystical Love[22].

The next two of the lists are of a different character.

9. The ninth is the historical **Buddha**, the 'founder' of Buddhism, whom Vishnu tries to re-absorb into one of his manifestations. However, this move is not one of conciliation and of orthodox acknowledgment of such a 'heretic' Sect, because the purpose adduced in the texts is stated to be "the mean to alluring the weak into falsehood for their ruin".

And

10. Kalki, the Horse Rider, is projected into the future. He is the final descent before the end of the Kali Yuga and the ultimate conflagration when all the universes would be again reabsorbed in their cosmic Unity. The figure of the equestrian animal would, by any chance, be intended as a remainder of the main royal Sacrifice as a hope for its creativity leading again to a future awakening?

o∗o∗o

As it could be seen, the "descents" of this exoteric expression of Brahmanic wisdom in the form of the Supreme God Vishnu are liable to be interpreted in many ways at different levels. From a 'cosmogonic' point of view they may be taken to outline the various degrees of evolution from matter, as Matsya and Kurma, to the highest Spirit as Krishna; from the psychological quest of perfection they can represent the steps the 'soul' has to go through climbing from the heaviness of the body up to the heights of Divine; and also, from a scholarly manner to consider the subject, as a device to 'brahmanise' the gods of those people that gradually came under the political, or simply cultural, influence of the 'Aryans'. A clear example of this, besides the figures of an Hanuman or a Ganesha drawn as lesser Deities in the bigger Pantheon[23], is Krishna himself who is seen as the highest expression of Vishnu while being obviously the God or/and king of Yadava folk—a population of cow-herders in the Mathura region near the Yamuna river. Krishna, in his own turn, is identified as Jagatnath (the Lord of the World) with the local Deity of Puri in Orissa, whose image is, significantly enough, attended by people belonging to a very low caste if not outcaste altogether.

Anyway, as often it is the case with creative Gods who have the tendency to become obsolete and retire into a *Deus otiosus* when their main task seems over, also Vishnu shows the same inclination of gradually lessening the worship due to his own figure as such, in favour of that performed in honour of his two most prominent Avataras, Rama and Krishna. Among the two, the latter is perhaps more interesting for his multifarious facets and his strange character dangerously at the bordering line of mischievious conduct, like many mythological entities all over the world. Right from the stories about his childhood and youth among the shepherds as related in the Puranas, up to his advises to the Pandavas, the heroes of the Mahabharata, his behaviour is quite reproachful and devious. He is a thief and a deceiver and urges his pupil and friend Arjuna to plunge mercilessly into a fratricide war disregarding sentimentalisms and a sense of guilt; and he is also a great lover, drawing to his fascinating youth all the female folk of his entourage regardless of the fact that most of them were married...including his greatest beloved Radha. This power of Love, which he enjoyed so much as to multiply himself into as many lovers as the Gobis (ladies shepherds) were, is what makes him the ideal recipient of Bhakti movement, or the Way of Mystic Love.

As a player of flute He is also connected not only with the world of the shepherds who traditionally play this type of musical wind-instruments (as for instance the God Pan in the Greek mythology), but also, esoterically, with the practice of Yoga. He shows, in fact, to the practitioners how to regulate and to direct breath so as to reach the seven Chakras—or points of energy—of the human body represented by the seven holes of the flute He held to his mouth. Besides, as Supreme God, He is connected with rain in its fertility aspect as well as in the violence of destructive storms and floods. The very black-bluish colour of his skin, referred to with the Sanskrit word Shyama, is the very colour of the sky when ready to pour down the terrific showers of tropical rainy seasons, when even his birthday is placed. Yet, it is rather his character of Protector that is emphasised also in these rather tense occasions, and He is known to have even uprooted a mountain for holding it up in order to provide shelter to people during one of such over aboundant pouring down.(14) However, as a Supreme Deity, he cannot be extraneous to the advent of birth and death, and in his Epiphany to

Arjuna, described in the Bhagavad Gita (ch. XI), his main and more striking activity is that of incessantly devouring the souls of people flying up into his mouth.

Yet, if in this most famous epiphany of Him there is a striking insistence on the most concrete aspects of life—He is said to have innumerable bellies, mouths, hands—and if in most of his myths He is depicted as a naughty boy or a restless youth given to the pleasure of earthly love, the poets chanting about him could not forget that they were dealing with the presentation of a Divine as rooted in the philosophical and mystical experience of the Vedas and especially the Upanishads. The Rishis of old had reached the unfathomable depth of What they called the Brahman, the impersonal Absolute, and the later poets, while converting this knowledge into popular stories and images easily graspable by the common, not initiated, folk, could not omit from time to time to let this 'Brahmanic Truth' surface. An example of such an occasion, besides the just mentioned well known revelation of Krishna to Arjuna, is a narration found in the (BrahmavaivartaP) in which the main God, Krishna again, together with Radha, presides a meeting of gods in his Heaven. All of a sudden a violent surging of cosmic Waters, dispersing everybody flying for shelter, floods the entire place. When, after calm is gained anew and the gods assemble themselves in a dry and safe land, with dismay they found out that Radha and Krishna were missing, they could not be comforted in their supposed loss, till Narada, the Pauranic bard, points out to them that They had not disappeared in the disaster, but They themselves were actually those Cosmic Water, whose real essence was the impersonal Absolute pervading everything in this primordial form. And Water is in fact the element associated with Vishnu when He rests on them at the end of every Yuga.

Somehow of a totally different character is the previous Avatara of Rama. Originally presented in the Epic bearing his name, the Ramayana, as a king (or rather a prince) hero, whose task was not much different from that of other Avataras of Vishnu—namely, that of the destroyer of Evil in the form of a Demon (in this case Rawana the King of Lanka), in a similar way in which Vamana came to get the world rid of Bali And Nara-Singha of Hiranya Kashipu—He was turned by the work of the poet Kalidasa of Benares into a proper God with all the characteristics of a Supreme Divinity, like Krishna. Actually, it seems, Kalidasa's was a move to counteract the popularity of the latter by presenting to the front another Avatara of Vishnu with a more 'respectable' character. Rama, accompanied by his wife Sita and one of his brothers, Lakshman, is the personification of Righteousness: obedient to his father wishes or whims up to self-denial and heroism, always serene, poised, self-controlled. He commands respect and love and even when killing his enemy maintains composure and detached equanimity. If Krishna is somehow the receiver of a turbulent, passionate Love from his devotees taking the feminine aspect of Radha and the Gopis, Rama on the contrary is the target of a more sober but not less absorbing dedication as represented more by the devout attitude of Hanuman, his follower by excellence, than by the quieter fidelity of his wife Sita, with whom he is coupled in cult and worship. Rama is rather the aim to be attained in meditation through the repetition of his salvific Name. And, as the myth shows, at a certain moment the power issued by his very Name becomes stronger even than Rama's will as such. As the story goes, at a certain moment Rama got angry with his very helper and devotee Hanuman and aimed at him with the darts of his bow, but he could not reach him because the armour provided by the repetition of the Name of Rama protected Hanuman![24]

Rama, too, in his own purified way, became somehow the means for 'brahmanising' local deities. Hanuman is the most outstanding example of this process. Officially belonging to a population of South-central India (Chota Nagpur) His most common and popular iconography is a stone roughly shaped in relief and painted in ocra colour (representing a reminder of an old and forgotten spread of sacrificial blood?) very similar to ancient 'tribal' idols not made by human hands but delineating themselves as epiphanies in the raw matter. And the fact that this type of image pertains to a previous and indepent cult is made unconsciously clear by the occurrence in Hanuman's shrines of either that epiphanic form standing alone as an independent object of human worship or by a secondary addition of the couple of his adoration (Sita and Rama) placed more or less in front of the primigenian idol; and this, in its turn, entinces a new presence of Hanuman in his Pauranic aspect. In such a way the final issue is that, in some of the, let say, 'primordial' or traditional shrines, both representations of the God are found[25]. Hanuman has the aspect of a tall monkey, the Langur type (tall, grey, with a long tail and a black face)[26], and is so taken up by the love he feels for rama and his wife Sita that he has their own images printed in his heart. He is strong and helpful so that when requested to bring a medicinal plant from the Himalays he found it easier to pick up the whole mountain itself so that the curer couldfind the medicinal herb himself. He is deeply loved by the Hindus for his power of granting wishes. He is worshipped especially on Tuesdays and Saturdays. His position in his religious branch of Hinduism is, then, similar (granting, of course, the differences due to their respective personalities) to that of Ganesha in the other branch. This God also holds a somewhat secondary or dependent position in the Shivaitic Pantheon—though enjoying the position of a son and not of a servant—and has a double iconography: the 'red stone' primeval idol and the moulded image adapted to his mythical figure as described in the Puranas.

The mention of Ganesha brings us to the description of the other main branch of Hinduism or popular Brahmanism: Shivaism, with its main God Shiva.

ii) Shiva

Different from the previous one as the night from the day is the Supreme Divinity of the second great branch of Hinduism: Shiva. This simile has not been assumed by chance. If, in fact, Vishnu represents the Day, Light, and the sun is his head flown to the sky, Shiva is connected with the Night, Darkness, and the Crescent Moon is lodged in his hair. Both, however, are not considered as the counterpart of one another or as two different faces of a single Unit or as complementary to each other as the diurnal and nocturnal aspect of Reality. Actually they are not interrelated, except in the artificially constructed Trimurti of which Shiva represents the Destructive Force. They are, each in his own right, an independent Supreme Principle impersonating two different ways of interpreting the universal and cosmic Truth. That the one is called to stress the luminous aspect of such a Truth and the other its somber and tenebrous side is only matter of their respective character and personality. Properly speaking, the whole Reality is represented by both and it is question of taste and inclination—both in the Gods themselves and in their priests and poets— that one aspect is stressed more than the other in each of the Hindu branches.

Altogether, Shiva has a strange and disturbing personality not easily to define. To begin with, He does not have a proper Name and all through his 'history' is mentioned with an attribute. Shiva actually is an adjective meaning: the Benevolent as a way of counteracting his frightfulness more or less in the same spirit in which the ancient Greeks used to mention the terrible Erynnis (representing Discord) as Eumenides (the Propitious ones). Even in the Vedic later texts, where He appears as the first response to a rising need of personal relationship of Devotion or Bhakti, his name is a generic Mahadeva, the Great or High God[26]. Furthermore, though his followers naturally enhance His position, His figure remains somehow in the borderline of the wilderness, the darker part of Reality, at the meeting point between Order and Chaos. He involves always a rather uneasy connection with the 'Unmanageable' in such a way that it was not difficult to assign to him the role of the Destroyer in the unifying concept of the Trimurti. As a God arising from the higher Vedic knowledge, He too, like Vishnu, could not avoid a connection with Sacrifice and its cultural World-view, but such a connection is ambivalent; the Bhaga, portion, reserved for Him is more akin to that allotted to the Demons than to that allotted to the Devas; and in one famous myth (to which a reference was made above when dealing with Pilgrimages) Shiva was so particular about receiving such a portion that He interrupted a sacrificial session where He was not invited in order to claim it, before destroying and polluting the whole performance[27]. In another myth, however, He manifests Himself as an endless Pillar of Fire, shooting up indefinitely toward Heavens and diving in the depth of a bottomless Underworld. In this way the myth asserts the superiority of Mahadeva over Vishnu and Brahma who found themselves unable to reach the respective limits of such Pillar: Brahma could not do it by flying in the above direction, while Vishnu, in his Varaha shape, could not dig as far into the profundities of below[28].

This manifestation of an Infinite Fire—also a fact that opposes Him to Vishnu, since the latter is associated with the cosmic Water on which He reclines during the resting periods between Yugas and on which He converts himself as Krishna, (as seen just above)—extending in both directions the above and the below, points out as well his double spiritual role in mysticism, leading the seekers toward the rarefied and subtle regions of Light and Heaven on one side, and towards the dark immensities of what in psychology is named Subconscious—or Unconsciousness. In this respect, the bipolarity and all in all the complexity of this Divine figure is made evident by seeing Him as the holder of opposing and contradictory extremes, in his conceptual as well as iconographic presentation. His features traditionally are that of a rather unkempt Yogi, with his long hair raised in a knot above his head but escaping all over on His shoulders; He is half naked and wrapped in a wild animal skin, with a cobra around his neck and sometimes also on his arms, sitting with crossed legs in a meditation posture on another animal skin (of a tiger or a dear); but crowning over such a rather rough and male appearance there is a face of a young girl, while his complexion is generally delicately white except for his throat which is blue because of the poison swallowed up during the 'churning of the Ocean'—another Puranic myth of creation[29]. This feminine trait in him on one side is the sign of the inner completeness of cosmic and human Reality and, on the other, contains a reference to his connection with the Shakti (feminine Power) in his task of creating, maintaining and finally destroying the phenomenal worlds. In fact, the Lord of the ascetics, dwelling in the solitude of the Mount Kailash peaks where He is absorbed in strenuous austerities (*tapasya*), is also strongly connected with the female part of Reality, either by leading a family life with his consort Parvati or Uma, or by incorporating Her in the composite figure of the Ardhanarishvara, the 'half-woman Lord', In His most famous and widespread 'aniconical' icon as male organ, the 'Linga', He is inserted in the feminine organ the 'Yoni'. In a more philosophical vision and especially in the Tantric way to spirituality, his feminine complementarily is the Shakti, creative Power, a personification of the Vedic sacrificial Ardour (called also Tapas), and representing the active Dynamism in the Universe. It is the Shakti of Shiva who eventually is responsible for the presence of the created worlds, but not, as one would be prone to think, through the 'natural' process of male-female unity—as it was the case with the Supreme Being of the Brahmanas, Prajapati. Here the Shakti, in her form of Kali, the Black One, acts alone through her dance, energised and almost intoxicated by the blood of the victims sacrificed to Her. And Her dance is performed over the inert body of Shiva, usual interpreted as the Spirit at the background of the dynamic whirling of Matter. In this case, the performance of the couple is the mythical parallel of the speculative presentation by the philosophical school of Samkhya of the interplay between Spirit and Matter, named Purusha and Prakriti. In this respect, the Shakti performances look rather independent activities altogether and, in cult, Shaktism (especially in some places like Bengal and the Mountains' regions, where the Great Goddess is worshipped under the names of Kali, Durga, and other of Tantric imprint), can be considered an autonomous branch of Hinduism loosely related with Mahadeva[30]. The Devi can be terrible, and more often than not, this is Her usual feature, so much so that often She is looked upon as connected with Death and put in charge of Destruction. What contributes to give such an impression is her being the usual receiver of the rare animal immolations still existing in India and Her images are often represented in the act of killing a Demon or of drinking blood from human skulls. But actually all these features stand for vitality and exaltation of life: blood and sacrificial killing are related to energy and increasing of vital power, while the fight of the Goddess is addressed against Demons and Evil thus making her a Protector rather then a Destroyer.

In this connection we may remark that it is very seldom, if ever, that a Supreme God would tackle Evil in a direct form. Either He does it by assuming different aspects in a lower level as in Vishnu's Avataras, or devolves this task to an intermediary Being as the Shakti. The story of the coming to be of Durga is significant in this respect: when Evil is again troubling the earth in the form of a Demon, the Devas seem helpless to face it. Thus they assemble and put forth their respective Shaktis or inner Powers so that out of all of them whirling together Durga concretises as a female. Once formed, She receives the personal attributes of the main Deities (the trident of Shiva, the charka—wheel—of Vishnu etc.) and becomes fit to fight Evil on behalf of the Divine (Devi Mahatmya, in Markandeya Purana)[31].

According to another Shivaitic myth, however, also well iconographically represented, Shiva alone is at the origin of the worlds through His own dance executed over the crouched body of a Demon who gives Him the material standing point. The images showing him in this creative act—starting with the rhythmical beating of the ritual drum, Damru, in one of His hands and ending in the consuming fire hold in another—do not only refer to the God's creative activity but also reveal the concern of the Lord of ascetics for the seekers of final freedom, by assuring them with a protective gesture of His third hand and by pointing out to them a way of escaping from the whirls of his dance with His last hand indicating the foot raised outwards. Shiva, in fact, as the Destroyer of creation is also the One who attracts the mystics seeking freedom beyond the binding revolutions of the wheel of life. And He does it not only through the path of renunciation and hard discipline aiming at reaching the Light of above, but also by plunging into the darkness of unfathomable psychological depth in order to find even there the hidden light of awakening. He is the God of intoxication.

As Mahadeva, He claims a no lesser connection with the Vedas and Brahmanas than Vishnu; and, though his connection with Yajna is not as clear-cut as that of the latter who won a contest over it, nevertheless it is strong enough if the Sukla Yajurveda makes him the receiver of a long and important oblation, so that He can be truly considered as belonging to the Vedic lore, culture and spirituality. As Rudra He is even already present in the Rigveda[32]. Yet, His character always at the border-line with darkness, fearfulness and even at time pollution makes him somehow the ideal link for representing non-aryan local folk and legitimising them into a 'lawful' interaction with divine Powers. After all, Gods as well have to be careful not to enter into an undue contact with the polluting power of Evil. Even in order to destroy it, they have to be properly screened. It is generally Shiva who takes over the task, in the same manner that it was He who dared swallowing the deadly poison issued by the already referred to Churning of the Milk Ocean. Accordingly, the main Demons and evildoers, opposed by Vishnu in his most important incarnations, generally are deeply religious persons and sound devotees of Lord Shiva. This fact was historically interpreted by considering Shiva the main Divinity of the Dravidians gradually becoming integrated into Brahmanic acculturisation. However, as it could be seen, the process could be also inverted and Shiva considered the Brahmanic figure that, for being at the cross point of many contrasting and opposing factors, could be a better fit agent for canalising local religious forces, (beginning, perhaps, with the so called Pasupati of Mohenjo Daro seal), which resisted the pressure of acculturation through Vishnuism and Krishnaism.

d. Comparisons

Vishnuism and Shivaism are definitely two different modes of popularising a cosmic and spiritual Truth which of old was experienced and elaborated into a highly philosophical and mystical knowledge. Yet, since their religious background was the same and also roughly the same were the existential situations to be faced, explained and made endurable, some parallels could be drawn between moods and characteristics that are found in the two groups. These connecting lines are not there to underlying a similarity, which is not and could not be there; but to reach a better understanding of the Truth these respective Divine Figures stand for. Though Vishnu, as seen, is rather on the side of the Day, the Light, Order and Righteousness, through Krishna He reaches also the darker half of Reality, the desire for freedom interpreted also as a wish to run away from the rigor of culture, Law and social strictness. Krishna is certainly not like Shiva Mahadeva in all respects; yet, He performs the same function of being at the borderline of Dharma not for the sake of an undue slip into a meaningless Chaos or of sponsoring a socially chaotic status, but as a manner to show the relativity of cultural patterns when the individual (and not society as a whole) seeks a higher spiritual realization. At his turn, Shiva, the Lord of ascetics (who are by definition those who have renounced this world and its rules) sets the example of a perfect 'family life' and often his iconography depicts him in a kind of "family portrait" together with his wife Parvati and their two sons: Ganesha and Kartikeya—if, however, both the sons are not regular issues of a couples normal behaviour, this is a different matter altogether[33]. Thus, the God whose inspiration to his devotees is that of disrupting family life by cutting links with 'samsaric' ties and relationships, cares also to present such relations as quite within the frame of legitimacy and mandatory relevance for the majority of humankind. He is the one who, officially, is presented as the Destroyer because He embodies the aspiration to spiritual freedom of the yogis and the ascetics. It is for their sake that Shiva seems to patronise, like Krishna, all what is devious from lawful but also worldly behaviour and, besides historical reasons bent to have him connected with local tribes which had to be brought under the cultural victory of a Rama or a Vamana, He is worshiped by the Demons that have to be defeated by Vishnuitic defenders of Dharma. Law and Order have finally to triumph for the welfare of life and society, and the seeker of spiritual freedom, though beyond this all, has to be made aware that his situation is anomalous and, if not properly checked in some of the excesses of his training, risks to slip into demonic behaviour instead of divine realization. But when Shiva is looked upon as Creator and Preserver of this world, then his destructive fury is turned against the evil forces bent to damage or interrupt the smooth course of events.

In this way, both Vishnu and Shiva, assisted by their respective cohorts of Gods and Goddesses (whom we did mention only in the notes in this cursory glance at the mentality behind the structure and growth of this diversified religious bulk named Hinduism), are meant to perform homologous function even if their respective approaches to life, culture and freedom from that all have different starting points.

Another way to better stress the different character between the two main Gods is by further widening the scope of comparison into at least one other Indo-European kinship. For this task the Greek religion presents itself spontaneously to mind if for nothing else for the fact that this very people automatically brought about some connections in the simple and natural endeavour to understand Indian experiences through their own—a task spontaneous to a polytheistic mentality. When first they came across Shiva, His behaviour and His cult, immediately they drew the parallel with their own God Dionysos. This Deity too was connected with freedom through drugs and intoxication, therefore through a lose behaviour meant to show indifference if not opposition altogether towards the rigid cultural laws of society. He too had a strict connection with the female section of humanity—normally kept in a subordinate position in cults—bearing a girl's face in the crude aspect of his rather wild features and, unlike Shiva, being attended by intoxicated women (the Menades) in his worship. Though absolutely Greek since the beginning of their culture (his name is found in the Minoic (Cretan) and Mycenaean civilizations) his position at the borderline of Righteousness and his propensity for a more popular stratification of society made him to be felt as 'foreign' to the more

Apollonian trend of Greek religion and his place of birth located in the
northern Tracia—like Apollo anyway—in the same manner as Shiva who
is often pushed outside 'aryanism' though not outside the territory of the
country. This sense of extraneousness is, then, not due to a real connection
with alien people (the Tracian for the Greeks and the non-Aryan
authochtons for the Indians) but rather to the unfamiliarity and the
Ganzanderen, the Totally Other, of a direct spiritual experience either
brought about by intoxication or by ascetic efforts and meditation.

On the other side, though Krishna as Supreme God patronises a similar
intoxication through Love instead of wine or drogue, He does not call for
such an association, even if free Love is not alien to his orgiastic behaviour
and that of his followers. What, instead, strikes the mind as a possible
approach are few but perhaps significant details, such as the connection
with the number 8 (being the 8th child of a persecuted set of brothers and
sisters, for instance), the colour in their complexion (blue like the rainy
sky) and by extension their connection with rain (though for Krishna this
connection does not extend to the lightning and thunderbolt). The figure
characterised by these not too marginal points is Zeus, the Greek head of
the Pantheon, and this is rightly becoming the main expression or the 8th
Avatara of Vishnu the more traditional representative of Brahmanical cultural
World-view. The Greeks however, mention Heracles has his homologeous.

The two different types of identification stress a clear line of
demarcation between the respective fields of 'specialization' of the heads
of the two main Hindu branches. Shiva as the God of abysses and the
highest experience (ungraspable on both directions as the myth of the
Pillar of Fire shows) is above culture because He stresses the other worldly
spirit of the intoxicated and of the philosopher who through highest
knowledge has freed himself from every bond; while Krihsna, though in
principle called to point toward the same direction of freedom, is an
incarnation of Vishnu who, through his Brahmanic contest, has identified
himself with the Vedic Yajna, representing Dharma par excellence, in the
same way as Zeus is responsible for Law and Order notwithstanding the
dubious morality of his Prajapati-like behaviour in his relationship with
women and girls human and Divine alike. As for what concerns Heracles,
he too is a strong and lawful Hero.

Thus, it may be said that in some respects we are faced with two
concrete interpretations of the cultural heritage of Aryan people, which
are deeply rooted in the wider human experience of the two main ways of
approaching the Divine: through the clear path of Law and Order and
through the more disturbing road toward the dark infinity outside 'civilized'

behaviour. India, however, from time to time adds to her sketching of Divine mythological personalities a reminder that the poets inspiration does not start from a forgotten source of a Pantheon of a 'past generation of Gods' (like, for example, the new arrangement brought up by the Greek Zeus when overcoming the 'old order' of his Father Kronos), but from the philosophical awareness and elaboration of the Upanishadic Seers who had reached the immeasurable Vastness of the Utterly Impersonal Absolute. Glimpses of such underlying vision have been related above in the narrations of Krishna's transformation into the Cosmic Waters and of Shiva's manifestation as an endless Pillar of Fire whose extremes could not be reached even by Divine efforts.

The other side of the coin is, then, the common awareness, as we have seen before, of the important role played by the realized human poets and seers in their position of 'creators' or 'moulders' of Myths. All through the various Pauranic and Epic narrations there are covertly, or sometimes even openly clear, repeated hints to the personal inspiration of the narrators in presenting that particular Divine figure and his or her way of reacting to a given situation. The Epics and Puranas have their recognized authors and even up till today the high Gurus and realized persons can present their version of the Divine with full authority. And not only them! Some ten or fifteen years ago a film-director created or rather promoted the worship of a 'new' Goddess—or, at least, spread at a nation wide level an originally regional cult—by presenting the story of a staunch devotee insisting in the worship of a seemingly 'non-existing' Goddess, Shantoshi Ma. In Heaven, the puzzled and envious three official Goddesses: the Vishnuistic Lakshmi, the Brahmanic Sarasvati the Goddess of Learning, and the Shivaitic Parvati, persecuted that devotee of an inexistent Entity. At the end Shantoshi Ma is forced to materialize herself in defence of her worshipper and in order to asserting herself before the other three. In spite of the evidence, the Goddess is accepted only when Narada, the Seer and Poet, explains to the four of them their common origin as aspects of the Shakti or Divine Power. The cult of the 'new' local Goddess spread to the whole of (Northern) India like a fire for some years.

As a counterpart of this liability in the Mythic figures, the Hindus are known as the only believers who can crack jokes about their Deities and their religious behaviour without being considered blasphemous, atheists or anti-religious positivists. And one can understand why it is so. Though both the Pantheons, from their Supreme Heads to the lesser gods, carry with them the highest Truth and even their respective iconography dealing with their external forms can reveal a deep philosophy within every detail, their inner Reality lays out of reach in the abstract of the Absolute. Whatever formal expression is given to It—the Sanskrit undetermined pronoun *tat*—can only be brought about by human mediation and does not carry the full weight of the "Thing in itself" and in this manner can also be treated lightly or seriously, with fun or seemingly disrespect. The same determinant role assigned to Rishis and Holy persons in general (even down to Film-directors!) presenting or sometimes 'creating' those very figures together with various degrees of interpretations according to the spiritual, psychological and emotional level of their audience contemporaries and of future generations) does not means—as it would be the case among 'modern' intellectuals—that religion is but a cultural human affair. What is openly recognised as cultural and contingent to human necessities of the moment is only the external shapes and manifestations, while warrant for their intrinsic validity is the trust commanded by the realised persons responsible for the narration of myths and of their always current interpretations. The importance given to Narada, the mythic singer and bard of the gods and humans alike is an example in hand.

But, then, an observer accustomed to a more fixed and 'reliable' religion may object, where a guiding line could be found which would not sway between evanescent dreamy or nightmarish images? How to get a firm, unshakable Truth in such a Divine fluctuating Reality? Or, in other words, how to reconcile a too multifold polytheism with the philosophical abstract vision of an abstract Divine, 'One without a second'? Or at least, since this is the situation presented in the texts, who is called to judge what is what and what should be the criterion behind choosing to worship one God instead of another? For an Indian such questions do not carry the same import than for the followers of monotheistic creeds or for the Westernised scholars. The latter, accustomed as they are to a monolithic (spiritual) Reality, are puzzled by a too drastic relativisation, which, according to them, could not have enough weight for sustaining a life-engaging religious attitude; for the former the issue is solved on an individualistic basis. The ultimate arbiter is the individual in spite of the bounds society imposes on him. The devotee, in fact, is the one who chooses and accepts his/her *Ista Devata,* that is the God of his/her choice for worship, and can also change the chosen God or Goddess for another One according to inner changes or the necessities of the moments.

NOTES

1. The literature on the subject is vast. Here there is a selection: S Bhattacharji, *Indian Theogony,* Kolkatta 1986; U Chakrovorty, *Indra and other Vedic Deities,*

New Delhi, D K Printworld 1997; R N Dandekar, *Vedic Mythological Tracts, Selected writings,* Pune (Bhandarkar Institute Press), 1979; A Danielou, *Le Polytheisme Hindou,* Paris (Buchet/ Chastel), 1960; W Doniger O' Flaherty, *Anthology of Vedic Texts.*

2. For general references see C J Bleeker and G Windengrens (edit) *Historia Religionum, Handbook for the History of Religions,* in 2 vols. Vol I *Religions of the Past,* Leiden (Brill) 1969.

3. Agni for Vishwamitra and Indra-Varuna for Vashishta.

4. See this feud especially Rig Veda III 53 and RV VII, 104 ending with the defeat of Vashishta, whose descendants took revenge in the epics degrading Vishwamitra to the rank if a Kshatriya conquering Brahmanhood.

5. See my article 'The role of ritual heat in Vedic sacrifice', Bijdragen,4/1978 Amserdam pp399-423.

6. In the Brahmanas are the Gods who perform the sacrificc; men are only copying what they peer at. See e.g. Ait Br VII 3(II. 2. 3.), f

7. See U M Vesci, *Heat of Sacrifice, op cit* Chap.II

8. See e.g. Sat Br VI 1 1 ff; X 4.2.2; and for a more detailed description L Silburn, *Instante et Cause,* Paris (Vrin) 1955.

9. See W Doniger O'Flaherty in her *Anthology of the Vedas.*

10. See Ait Br XII. 10 (III.2.2) and a variant in Taitt Br II.2.1.1 f

11. See my article 'Kah, le nome de Dieu comme pronome interogatif' in Archivio di Filsophia, ed E Castelli, Rome 1968

12. fn.: we do not wish to commit ourselves to any external chronology and we can refer to, only as a kind of reference point, that in the opinion of scholars this period is tentatively put around the Xth and IXth centuries BC

13. Fn: see e.g. my experience in Rajasthan where even brahmans and very religiously committed people never heard of the existence itself of such a branch of Vedic literature

14. See e.g. D Kinsley *Hindu Goddesses. Visions of the divine feminine in the Hindu religious tradition,* Delhi Motilal Banarasidas 1987 (Org. Calif. Uni. Press 1986)

15. See my quoted book chapt.8 pp220 ff

16. See e.g. N Aiyangar *Ancient Hindu Mythology* Delhi Deep Publication 1983 pp513ff

17. In this case the occasion is to provide a firm ground for the "Churning of the Ocean", a myth very important in Puranic religion, which we could not talk about. See Bhagavata Purana, VIII 5.15ff; Vishnu Purana VI 1.9.30ff etc.

18. In other mythologies of the wold this function is performed by a bird, see M Eliade, *De Zalmoxis a Gengis Khan,* Paris, (Payot), 1970 Chapt. III.

19. This Story is reported in many Puranas and its recitation is commonly connected with the celebration of Holi. See above

20. This ritual is prescribed in the Sat Br VI.6.4.1 ff; Katya SS XVI.5.11ff; etc., though at that time neither Vishnu nor such myths were involved.

21. Rama, the perfect king and hero of the epic Ramayana, through the performances of his exploits in the sacred play, Ramlila, has spread over east and southeast Asia; see R P Goldman, "The Ramayana and the problem of an 'Asian' cultural area; Valmiki's values in India and beyond", in Purana, Varanasi (All India Kashi Raj Trust), Jan 2003 pp7ff. See later about his personality.

22. A great deal of the Puranas are centered on this figure. See e.g. Bhagavata P. Brahma Vaivarta P. he is also the main hero in the Mahabharata culminating in his revelation in the Bhagavad-Gita.

23. The figures to be presented later are still the main deities of tribal groups. Hanuman worshipped in Chotta Nagpur Jharkhand and Ganesh on the western Coast.

24. Towards the end of the Ramayana

25. I witnessed this case in a shrine in Varanasi.

26. See Svet. Up. Passim and Yajur Veda XVI called the shatarudrya i.e., the litany of his hundred names.

27. See above

28. This myth is incarnated in the southern mountain Arunachala in Tamil Nadu; the recurrence of this 'vision' is celebrated every year during the full moon after Dipawali by kindling an enormous fire in its top

29. This myth uncovered here has been mentioned in the footnote 17 in the IInd avatara of Vishnu

30. See D Kinsley op cit

31. See her coming into being and her exploits in the Devi Mahatmya taken from Markandaya P. and recited during equinoxial festivities.

32. See RV, 1.114.1-5; RV VII, 46.1-4; etc.

33. We have not presented these gods as yet.Katikeya is a 'product' f Shiva and is the mythical expression of the cosmic Khambha or Pillar (AV X.7.1ff); he has six heads and bear his name from the fact that in the myth at his birth he was fed by the six stars of the Kartika constellation (the Pleiades). His brother Ganesh is fashioned by Paravati (Shiva's consort) out of the sandal paste smeared on her body. The boy was made in order to guard and protect her from the lust of her ascetic husband. Furious of the obstacles cut off his head but repenting replaced it with that of an elephant (the first being found sleeping with its head towards the north) See Shiv P. and others. As already seen he too like Hanuman is represented as a roughly self shaped stone painted in red beside its usual iconographic murtis.

PART IV
SPIRITUAL DIMENSION

CHAPTER 1
The domain of the individual

1. Religious demand of individuals

The sentence ending the previous chapter seems to be in contradiction with what has been said about the great role played by community life and society in the Indian manner of conceiving existence. Besides, it is generally agreed upon that the concept itself of *individuus* is the Western product of Renaissance fully developed during Illuminism, while getting inspiration from the words of the Master of Nazareth, the Christ, who maintained for the first time the possibility for a person to be 'saved' by himself and not through the common salvation promised to the 'people of Israel' as such. In the same way, Indian society is so collectively organised that even the word for individual is unknown. Every person, in fact, is born conditioned by being inserted into a given family, *gotra* or *gens*, caste, village, region, and even religious tradition of his forefathers; and, till he becomes at his turn the head of his family group, he is subjected to the authority of his father, mother and elder brother. A person behaving independently from all these conditioning factors is generally unthinkable, except...if he cuts it all by becoming a spiritual seeker, a *samnyasa*. In this case he is legitimated to be alone.

The very fact that a stage in life, that accepts this type of severing social bondage, not only exists but is given the highest place in human spiritual goals, bears a far greatest importance in bringing along, side by side the high value enjoyed by society, the idea of personal responsibility in one's own inner development and salvation. A fact that has always disturbed the 'individualistic' religions of Jewish derivation (Christianity, Islam and even the secular Marxism) and Buddhism too, is that the Hindus, wrapped as they are in social conditioning, are salved alone; while the individuals severed by their national and racial commitment but regrouped into a different type of Communities (Ecclesia, Umma, Sangham), are considered responsible also for the other members of their respective groups and cannot even think to be saved alone. Their salvation is in the community (see the Christian dictum: *extia Ecclesia unlla salus*)

But, if salvation is a strictly personal problem, an obvious corollary goes with it: the individual should be extremely important and at the centre of every spiritual and even social concern. And actually it is as such, in spite of the great emphasis given to the role played by social and communal interchanges and bondages. In a country where everyone depends on everyone else, up to the moment when old age and wisdom give him (or her) a place of authority, and practically privacy does not exist at any level, I was tempted to title a planned work on Indian culture (the result of my first impact with this land): "in the country where one hand washes itself", adapting to the occasion a well known Western proverb. This title would not only properly reflect an actual physical situation—one hand being busy in holding the pouring vessel in a place where tap water is not always available—but also the lack of cooperation in the trivialities of life exhibited by these too compenetrated social people. This is because, perhaps just for counteracting the psychological pressure of such a situation, each person is felt and considered as the very centre of every experience, as the only one responsible for what he succeeds in doing with his own life, regardless of his conditioning situations. Often, one is left with the impression that the elders' pitiless demands imposed to the younger members of the family or of the clan is, consciously from the part of a guru, unconsciously in a lay society, but a mean to force the individual to react and to become aware of his inner personality and intrinsic independence.

The cultural end result of this mixed way of looking upon human presence in this world—as member of a community and as an individual fully responsible for his inner growth—is the extreme variety of personal reactions to a relatively limited mode of existential situations. To such uniqueness in human beings the Guru addresses himself when called upon to guide his disciples (never considered as an indiscriminate group), while the wise elders and priests keep it in mind when elaborating the cultural patterns of existence. This experience, centred on individual behaviour and psychological reactions, grows step by step passing through various levels of 'living realities', so that there is a kind of widespread feeling that the extremely elaborated and refined social and ritual systems are but an external organization of existence in order to protect the individual against his 'ontic' solitude, but that it has to be overcome when he is lead to gradually accept such solitude and to assume it in full awareness.

In this sense, that is as seen from the point of view of the growth of the single person, the philosophers speak about the world of sensorial experiences as *samsara*, i.e. the "wheel of life", ceaselessly revolving around cycles upon cycles of space and time in a sequence of real and concrete actions (because charged with real consequences in the process of unfolding life as to constitute those 'blocks of Karman' we have already spoken about in a previous chapter), but revealing themselves as emptied of inner value as the empty sound of an insect in a close hive, to the sage who had the strength of transcending such situation in the solitary path of his self-realization. However, the way to inner growth is long, full of difficulties and inner psychological resistances, both on the part of the individuals who somehow feel comfortable inside their human mould, and on the part of society which does not want to loose its hold on its members. Brahmanism, when bridling reality in a series of rituals and cultural order, was also helping the individuals as such to proceed in their path toward 'salvation' by giving them direction and support in their walk through repeated social and religious landmarks. But when some of them, in their pushing forward, reached a stage of advanced personal independence, then the same orthodox tradition allows them to cut their ties with society and with its cultural setting in order to pursue their proper spiritual path in freedom and solitude.

Useless to say, however, that when the individual sets on his way to freedom from life-conditioning he is still far from his goal so that yet needs guidance, landmarks and support, though these had to take obviously a more personalised standard. To this respect, tradition, recognising the almost infinite variety of human feelings, psychological tendencies and of the different levels gradually attained by the seekers, offers them three specialized walks, paths—in Sanskrit: *margas*—to follow in their quest, each emphasizing a special mood or attitude in character. It also presents the seekers with the possibility of conceiving and following in a vast range of forms the Divine goal they are after. Thus, the individual quest can still claim a kind of order while, at the same time, acknowledging the personal exigencies of each 'walker'.

CHAPTER 2
The Three Spiritual Ways or Margas

The traditional spiritual ways are called, from the emphasis put on their mode of approach to their respective goals, the Path of Action, of Knowledge and of Love or Devotion, that is, in Sanscrit terminology: the Karma, Jnana and Bhakti Margas. They appear to be acknowledged as far back as the Yajur Veda and the Brahmanas and they alternate in the course of time becoming fashionable in different moments of history in a kind of an irregular recurrence. Each coming into fashion again brought with it as a natural consequence new addings, new interpretations and a new spirit according to the mood of the times. Since in India, as it has been said, history is not measured following precise events settled in a given time, it is difficult for external observers to distinguish the various contributions proper to each revival. However, the preference given to one of such paths did not mean that the other two were totally disregarded; they were only pushed to the background and left to those who still found them more congenial to their characters and inclinations in spite of being considered 'out of the current fashion'.

Somehow, perhaps, it is only by sheer chance that the alternate coming to the fore of one particular Marga at the expenses of the popularity of the previous in the line often coincide with the political uprising of a caste or a class over the others and that the contributions introduced at each coming back in fashion are strangely related with the mentality prevailing in the social group raised to power, or imposing the awareness of their conditions to the ruling class. Just anticipating an example, it could be said that the Karma Marga, the first that can be recognised in the Scriptures, as the Way of Action, put emphasis on the ritual essence of Brahmans' Activity and required a joined power of kings sustained by priests and priests leaning on kings for support and for legitimising their own authority. When, after centuries, priestly prestige became too extracting the vexed Kshatriyas decided to shift the emphasis of ritual performances into an equally valid spiritual way based on the theoretical Knowledge of their inner power. The way of Knowledge became, then, the leading mark of the spiritual seekers whatever their social origins. Yet, this Marga, pursued by noble spirits, was soon judged too difficult for the average man who became to assert his needs as far back as the time of the Bhagavad Gita, and the way of Devotion, as surrendering one's strives to the mercy of God, came to be considered as more suitable for a larger number of individuals, together with a return of the Karma Marga in which the Action involved was, by the time of the same Gita, shifted to the secular activities of the seekers as well as of common people. History has known through centuries various resurgences of the three till nowadays, when the gurus are attempting a synthesis of all of them.

A closer look to each Marga, presented in the chronological order that more or less was followed in history, will confirm what has been hastily sketched above.

a. Karma Marga

It is the first Marga in a chronological as well as religious sense, since is found, as stated above, right from the Brahmanic sacred literature, and that is why, perhaps, it has a long, diversified and complex history behind itself, though not always free from blame on the part of the followers of other spiritual paths. It is also, as just seen, the one which, due to its slow penetration into all the different layers of population, has more radically changed the object of its search and, therefore, also of the mean to obtain perfection through it. The very word Karman has gone through various levels of content while gradually penetrating into larger and less privileged layers of society.

At the beginning of its 'career', as it were, Karma is applied to the Sacred Action, Yajna, the only activity worthy of such name, and its literature are the Vedas, especially the hymns and their Brahmanas. Since, from ancient time onward, the accepted goal of such type of cult is to obtain concrete results and advantages in this very world (as it has been discussed some chapter above), the philosophy and World-vision attached to it could not help but being positive, appreciative of life brought forth and reinforced by its very performance. Not by chance its divine representative in the exoteric religion is Vishnu, the Preserver. Such a positive concern with the concrete world of existence is prolonged on the 'other world' too, since in his performing of a sacrificial cycle, a Yajamana acquires for himself and for his wife, together with the immediate aim of a particular Yajna, also an immortal body able to be transferred, after the apparent death of the material body, in the heavenly Svarga, Paradise. It goes without saying that, in this very personal ritual Action, side by side the immortal transformation of its sponsor, the entire reality acquires solidity, is transformed and becomes immortal, thus reaching divine steadiness. As shown before, the strength inherent to this Action is so powerful that it draws into its orbit even the Gods, who, with time and further philosophical development, are called upon to obtain their own immortality through the same ritualistic means. In this way, Karma Marga is the path moving on the direction pointed out by classical rituals, transferred for daily use to domestic cult, as a way of creating, transforming and stabilising life, into a solid, energetic and immortal reality. Traditionally, as seen at its proper place, such Marga is compared with the action of Weaving, thus allowing, also in a personal and individualistic manner, to display one's own weft within the dharmic frame of social warp, all brought about through the active mediation of the priests.

Nevertheless, this way toward realization of one's own nature was not always free from difficulties and even opposition. To begin with, some difficulties were arising right at the core of sacrificial rites which resulted in the awareness of the existence of a diffuse and no longer checkable Pain in creation. Such a discovery lead to the Upanishadic, Jain and Buddhist reaction bent to drop sacrifice altogether, thus abstaining from perpetuating a life full of unavoidable suffering[1]. With passing of time, such objections became stronger also among the traditional section of society, which stressed further on the importance of spiritual knowledge as a better means to attain spiritual perfection. This is the Path of Knowledge, the Jnana Marga, which shall be considered below. On another level, with the rising of self-awareness among the average larger strata of population, enjoying indirectly the material advantages of this Yajnic path but not its spiritual perfecting possibilities, such religious activities forming the backbones of Karma Marga, began to be looked askance as too specialized and too discriminating to be considered a widespread means to spiritual realization. The reaction to it, developed keeping in mind the necessities of such people who, though attracted by spiritual freedom, could not discard Action, Karma, either as a personal inclination or as a need for supporting their lives and that of their relations, was to retain the powerful drive of Action as such, applied to secular rather than ritualistic activities, and turning it into an effective tool for reaching individual 'salvation' or 'realization'.

Both shifts of emphasis, however, could not occur without carrying with them also a drastic change in the spiritual, and therefore also cultural and philosophical perspective of human attitude in and toward this world. Since Karma—and it does not matter much if ritualistic or secular—is bound, as seen before, to bear durable consequences in human as well as earthly existence (a position which was not objected to in Vedic times, but rather cherished and fostered), any attempt to still use it as a means to spiritual realization needed first to purify it and to turn its drive, antithetic to spirituality, into an 'harmless' performance—harmless in so far as prevented from producing lasting concrete effects. To this purpose, it was suggested, from Bhagavad Gita[2] onward, to change the inner attitude toward it so that whatever action was chosen as a vehicle for proceeding along this Marga had to be done with perfect skill, dedication and concern but without any attachment or expectation for its results and fruits. In this manner, the attention and concentration put into it would help the doer to perfect himself, while lack of attachment would deprive activity of its main drawback: its capacity to produce an endless chain of effects and counter-effects and thus perpetuating the conditions the seeker attempt to escape from. And this is as difficult as any other spiritual path so that, in spite of being promoted by such an authority as the Bhagavad Gita, fell quick out of fashion and only recently, pushed forward by 'modern' mentality, inclined more to activities and utility for others than to quietness, begins to enjoy a kind of revival.

b. Jnana Marga or the Path of Knowledge

This spiritual Path also goes back as far as Vedic, or at least late Vedic, age and is often presented as an intellectual reaction to a too restricted and too stiff ritualistic mentality and to more and more dry ritualistic performances. Its 'inventors' or at least staunch promoters are the Upanishadic sages themselves, of whom some are Kshatriyas that is, belonging to the ruling class. There is, indeed, no doubt that this last portion of Vedic literature provoked a kind of 'revolution' with respect to a religion which bestowed great value to ritual action as a mean to produce creation as well as to improve, transform and immortalize it through further repetitions. Nevertheless, one would be more correct to call it a kind of 'involution' because, though sounding radically in opposition to the past, in reality it was more in line with an inner development than the product of a drastic cut. For one thing, the 'heroes' of this 'revolution' were the same stead-fast ritualistic authorities who were consulted in the Brahmanas whenever some problems of interpretations arose; from the other, the move toward a shift in emphasis from the proper action to its inner knowledge as equally powerful for reaching the expected results were already implicit in the reiterated Brahmanic affirmation that "one becomes what one knows"[3]. Besides, the slide to interiorization should have been smooth as shown by the famous dialogue between the king Janaka and his chief priest Yajnavalkya, the authority of the Satapatha Brahmana, who was brought by his ruler and patron to gradually acknowledge the possibility that, failing to have milk for the Agnihotra's main offering, this ritual action could be yet performed with the inner offering of one's own intention and abstract self[4].

This path, stressing even more the individual effort on the way to salvation and freedom from the snare of phenomenal worlds, is, in its early stages, an almost natural deepening of the necessity of a profound and detailed knowledge about the meaning, scope and attainments of solemn rites. From there to a final and explicit emancipation from the actual sacrificial performance to an interiorised and sublimated meditation on its spiritual effects the step was not too long and, perhaps not by mere chance, was pushed forward by the kingly class as an alternate way of supplying missing offerable items. Moreover, just to stress a little further the continuity with Vedic ritualistic tradition, it is not out of place to remind oneself that it was part of a custom going far back into the past, the habit of retiring at a certain age from active life and devoting the rest of the existence to deepening the theoretical and spiritual implications of the rites and cults previously performed. Thus, in a certain sense, it would be easy to surmise that Jnana Marga would have had its normal place in the smooth running of the traditional life without producing much ado.

Yet, it would be difficult to deny that, though somehow the 'logical' consequence and development of the ritualistic Karma Marga, the Way of Knowledge has produced such radical alterations of religious behaviour as to change its very goal together with the philosophical World-view attached to it. Following their quest for freedom through inner self-Examination, the seekers of Knowledge kept on discovering unsuspected depths in the Absolute and inconceivable possibilities for their own selves to merge with it. Their answer to the solicitations of the traditionalists was that the latter's way was narrow and limited, not conducive to the 'real' destination of Man: his total freedom into the Spirit.

They argued, and mostly the results of such arguing was collected in the last chapters of the Brahmanas later divided as the Aranyaka and especially the Upanishads, that while ritual Karma was bound to perpetuate the chain of Karmic effects into a continual creation and preservation of these worlds however detached they could be, abstract Knowledge had the advantage of getting straight at the source of that creation. But a not minor consequence of this direct Path toward interiorisation is a reverse evaluation of Nature and Reality which could as well account for the feeling of revolt and opposition going along with its presentation: while aiming directly to the Spirit what is concrete, multifarious, heavy matter (including the seeker's body) become an obstacle that has to be overcome if not destroyed altogether; destroyed or perhaps better melted away before a newly acquired awareness of its lack of ontic existence. Seen with respect of the geographical space surrounding the Jnani, (the follower of this type of Way), his attempt to reach Reality without the intermediary of its cultic and cultural interpretation, pushes him directly to face the Void opening behind the chaotic exuberance of the Tropics. A straight glimpse of this kind is hard to hold for an intrinsically finite being, because of its immensity, and the only manner to stand its impact is avoiding measuring individual 'nothingness' with It and disappearing in It by letting go of one's personality and self. "To become what one knows" attains its culmination when the goal of that 'knowing' is the Unknowable par excellence, which claims for such a so called 'privilege' the total price of one's very self as an independent and finite entity.

No wonder, therefore, if even this Marga, like the previous one, elicited objections from different quarters: from the multitudes still attached to the lure of this very world that consider it too drastic, and from other seekers of the Spirit appalled by the harshness of asceticism involved for proceeding on it and by the immensity of the price to be paid at its end. Due to the utterly Impersonal character of the perceived Absolute the walker on this path cannot expect any external—supernatural—help and has to curb his personal character, with its inclinations and idiosyncrasies, through self-imposed discipline and self-control. Very soon the Jnanis, notwithstanding the awe-inspiring admiration and respect they commanded with their inner poise, serenity and detached behaviour and in spite of the high esteem amounting almost to worship bestowed on the sacred texts transmitting their wisdom (the Upanishads), found themselves rather isolated and less and less in number. As often it happens in society, in any society, even a religious one, if 'something'—it does not matter what and at what a price has been attained—appears to belong to a minority and such a minority seems to enjoy it to a good degree, immediately it is looked upon by the 'excluded' ones as a privilege hold by what is equated with an "aristocracy". In the case of spiritual seekers such label of aristocrats has also the historical support of Upanishadic tradition, whose main teachers (gurus) were Brahmin Purohitas or, as just seen, kings. Practically, however, their high-standard status has nothing to do with caste or class's connection. At that level it is personal attainment which counts and, though traditionalists do not hide their preference of following the low procedure of reaching Brahminhood before jumping out of society altogether, actual facts prove sufficiently enough that Jnani 'aristocrats' may also have socially emerged even from out-caste groups[5]. Anyway, the objections to this Way to Freedom are addressed to its extreme difficulty which makes it *ipso facto* the choice of very few. The Man of Knowledge wants Freedom and acts on his own to obtain it. The way of his preference has been traditionally compared with that exhibited in nature by the monkey-babe, who since the beginning is made responsible for his own status. Since his mother has to move freely among trees (or roofs in Indian cities), she cannot be bothered by holding the babe; it has to stick to its mother with its own strength and grasp. In the long run, this attitude may be tiring for those who are not sustained by their own inner determination, especially when the odds of one's characters or the difficulties of the path paved the road with failures.

An alternate way comes forward when, possibly under the impact of such failures, a feeling of helplessness creeps on among the weaker people. The religious personalisation of the philosophically discovered Brahman into exoteric Gods and Goddesses was, perhaps, instrumental in presenting such an alternative. To a discouraged disciple, or to a dejected seeker could be a solace to turn to an understanding Divine figure and plead for help. This trust on someone powerful enough to take over the lack of self-confidence in a subject could be a welcome way out from trouble and can be found already in a later Upanishad (SvetUp) where the Saviour is Mahadeva. However his boom as a much advertised and apparently easier way to Salvation occurs a bit later and became popular among the less (spiritually) privileged people especially through the figure of Krishna, from the Gita onward.

c. Bhakti Marga or the Path of Love or Devotion

Also the coming forward of this new way to an inner Realization is marked with a sense of 'revolution', of opposition to the intellectually better es-tablished Way of Knowledge. Though at the beginnings possibly only a temporary support and a needed redressing of one's diminished determi-nation and thus seen as rather a kind of remedy, soon the overpowering personality of the Divine began to strike back and not only to present this Path to Freedom as the highest, but also to look down to the previous in line as based on pride and self-esteem. In fact, it was reasoned, what did man think himself to be before the Almighty Divinity? Is he not less than earth beneath God's feet? How then can he claim to rely only on his inner resources for reaching perfection? Will it not be the highest of presumptions on his part? On the contrary, to recognise one's own helplessness and to lay oneself to the feet of the Lord asking for mercy and support thus placing full trust in His high Power is both a manner to avoid self assurance and pride and, comparatively, a less difficult path to move along in. In contrast to the way of the babe-monkey, actively involved in cooperating with its mother, the seeker preferring this attitude of trust and abandon is compared to the behaviour of kittens: in order to be moved from one place to another they have only to relax completely and let their mother hold them by their scruff. Such should be, then, the inner disposition of the Bhakta, the loving devotee: complete trust and full relaxation. God would do the rest.

Besides, with respect to the previous path to Realization loaded to the brim with harshness and discomfort and, on top of everything, leading toward the nullification of the seeker's personality merged in the Absolute, the Way of Love and Devotion has the advantage (for a certain type of mentality) of keeping alive individual souls (*atman*). Their existence as separate entities is prerequisite for establishing a permanent relationship between a Lover, the Divinity, and his Beloved, the mystic. Love is possible, likewise worship and adoration, only if there are two differentiable poles allowing 'Something' similar to an electric charge to pass through and fro. What is overlooked, however, by those luring themselves to suppose this way easier than the other two is that, even if the relationship requires a polarity and in spite of the fact that the main individual responsibility is taken away from the weaker member of the couple, in order to fulfil mystical expectations the Lover claims absolute surrender from the Beloved almost to the point of forgetting one's separate personality. Though Love's invocations use the pronoun Thou implying diversity, only if the mystic transfers his total awareness in the contemplation of the Lover can his happiness be effective, but in this way even if theoretically his 'ego' continue to be a distinguished entity, it is totally forgotten in the effort of projecting it into the Object of its Love.

At this stage, when Love has accomplished the marital mystic union to a highest degree, the sage does no longer need to engage himself in the worship of the image of his chosen form of God or Goddess, or in endlessly repeating the Divine Name. Whatever help he derived from the nama-rupa required for his still imperfect senses, it should cease to exercise its hold once the Lovers have merged in a permanent perfect bliss. Nevertheless, to reach this apex the way is long and at moments as hard as any other. It is in fact well and good to surrender and leave the initiative and responsibility of one's salvation to the Divine counterpart, but in spite of inner desire egotistic personalities do not let themselves go without struggle and just relaxing into the Hands of God is not so 'natural' as for the kitten. The *sadhana* of the Bhakta can be, at times, as hard as that required in the Path of Knowledge and also implies as much detachment as asked from the Man of Action in his physical toils not supported by expectation of results.

Bhakti Marga is chronologically the latest attempt of individuals in their struggle to reach Salvation. It enjoyed several upraises and it appeared specially fitted to counteract the influence of Islamic mysticism. Its popularity came also to the fore when larger and less learned strata of population acquired social influence or their spiritual unattended needs began to prickle into the consciousness of monks and gurus, the responsible people for cultural and religious settings. Over against the rigidity of Brahmin priests busy in defending the purity of their temples, popular stories began to circulate showing worshipped images turning on their axis to face the humble prayer of an out-caste woman not allowed inside the premises[6] or the sudden barring of a road by a cast-off leper preventing a 'pure' Brahmin to continuing on his way. To the insults of his disciples urging the unclean man to clear the way the latter turned out to be nothing less than an epiphany of Lord Vishnu[7]. And, as strange as it may seem to those who consider Shiva the patron of the 'locals', the Dravidians and non-Aryans in general, the defender of the rights of the socially despised ones is usually Vishnu either in his own form or as Krishna. Direct Love does not need cultic restricted paraphernalia or the discriminative intermediary presence of priests, together with the salvific knowledge of Sacred Texts. Anyone, with good will and strong determination, may directly approach the Divine, under whatever form a fluid polytheism would provide, and trust its mercy. And as pupils for this path can arise from whatever social background, so also gurus do not need to proceed only from the Brahmanic lore. Whoever got so much stamina to overcome his pettiness and to merge into the Absolute (either by being absorbed by Its impersonality or by being lost in a Love embrace) has by the same act acquired the perfect Knowledge and the right dimension for becoming a spiritual teacher and a valid authority for (re)interpreting culture at the light of new historical needs. But all this is not easy and even in order to be able to accept and get benefit from the help of God the Bhakta has to undergo a hard training (*sadhana*) more or less in the same way as the Jnani, while for both the Way of Action is somehow discarded as it seems to have been considered a lower stage.

d. Yoga

The rescuer, so to speak, of the value of the body, even if not of the matter as a kind of appreciation for the phenomenical world, can be considered the Path of Yoga, in its many branches. Connected with the Samkhya system of philosophy, it views Reality as composed by Spirit (the Purusha) and Matter (Prakriti); the former rather static, immobile as at rest but stirred into movement by the unceasing activity of its feminine counterpart, the Shakti whirling into concreteness as Prakriti. Obviously also Yoga is the child of post-upanishadic mentality and the main aim of its practices is to still down the movement of Matter so as to allow the Purusha to recover his peace and balance. Nevertheless the way toward this goal is not by deny the material aspect of the World nor by humiliating the body, but to assume it and work through it till moulding it into a perfect health and a superb control over its functions, feelings and reactions.

The very term denoting it hints[8] at what Yoga is bent to pursuing: a harmonious junction between body and spirit in a combined effort of a common growth. However, even along this path the final result is a victory of the Spirit who eventually will take over when the body has been silenced into immobility of muscles and of thoughts. The positive value bestowed on this very world according to the World-view arising from the Karma Marga supported by cultic rituals, seems lost for ever for the mystics wishing to still down the glamour of worldly life and to escape the cyclical endlessness of births-deaths-rebirths...Yoga, however, especially in its Hatha Yoga branch, has also physical health within its range and though eventually bent to quench desires and creative movement does not pull out its followers from worldly life, at least not in the drastic ways fostered by the Jnana and Bhakti Margas.

o*o*o

At this point a warning is of the essential before closing this chapter. Individual paths and quests not necessarily take the direction of Samnyasa and Renunciation. Individuals can also be engaged in pursuing their perfection (because such is, normally, the drive carrying their activities—or

lack of them—on) within a mundane scope (career, refinement of character, social success and the like) but in this case their personal striving is
framed within society and its rules, and they have been dealt with in the
bulk of this exposition. The personal struggle stretches along several
lives wrapped inside society and institutions, caste system and work's
opportunities, thus being deeply influenced and determined by them.
Nevertheless, from time to time, few individuals are singled out, in every
living situation, by their specific ways to react to conditioning factors.

Here, however, we have stressed the spiritual paths because these
are where individuals really move alone, according to their inner bent of
character, inclinations and also 'vocation', even purposefully and willingly
disentangling themselves from social and religious fixed patterns and
cultural protection. The holy man, the sage, the seeker is the clearer example
of solitary struggle toward the awakening of the spiritual dimension;
conversely, spirituality is essentially a personal conquest and concern (an
opinion that hold true in almost every religious, philosophical and social
World-view) and its quest is pursued mainly outside cultural frames,
paradoxically even outside properly organised religions. This does not
forcefully means that mystics and mystical aspirants have as a rule to
withdraw from actual life, leave society and retire to secluded spots. Mostly
they do it because ordinary concerns have faded away from their interests,
though from time to time one can come across realizing and realized people
and gurus still apparently merged into family and worldly life. Yet, the
specification "apparently" is not out of place because, though still busy
around, their degree of detachment keeps them free in their own egoless
atmosphere.

It has to be add that, on ground of expediency, the seeker and realized
person have been spoken upon in a masculine gender, simply because
this very gender is omni-comprehensive (at the contrary of the feminine
one which refers only to subjects of this species). Actually the female per
cent of people engaging themselves in all the mentioned paths is rather
high and even higher is the average number of realized souls belonging to
the womanly half of mankind... and not only in modern times when women
have almost succeeded in achieving social equality. Gargi, Mirabhai,
Anandamayma, Krishnabhaima, Amrtanandamayma, are only but few name
on a long list.

At this point a warning is of the essential before closing this chapter.
Individual paths and quests can not always take the direction of Samnyasa

NOTES

1. See my art. "The role of Ritual Heat in Vedic Sacrifice". (The place of pain in the
   act of creation) "in Bijdragan Leiden 4/1978 pp 399-423, where it is shown that,
   during ritual performances painrises as an unavoidable element in creation.

2. Bhagavad-Gita is among the earlier texts which detached Karma from sacrifice and considers it applicable to the common action equal to work of any human being.
3. A repeated formula at the end of every explanations of given yagnic rituals especially in Sat. Br. Passim
4. See Sat. Br. XI.3.1.1.24 already quoted.
5. At the start of my stay in India around the early sixties I was informed about the existence of a youth who was in permanent samadhi (deep meditation) under a tree of jnanic type and belonged to a very low caste.
6. This is a story referring to a Vishnu Temple in southern India
7. Kabir
8. From the Sanskrit root Jug meaning to join.

CHAPTER 3
Their Ultimate Equivalence

It emerges, from what presented above, that practically only two ways or attitudes are open to Indian people when whishing to assert their personality without risking loosing their mind or their way in the overwhelming intricacies of a too exuberant tropical nature, whose vastness itself is instrumental in letting the inherent cosmic Void pop up from time to time. These modes are: to accept to be guided within the cultural and cultic frames woven by society through its traditional religious coordinates, thus surrendering individual freedom in exchange of security, order, the warmth of close human relationship; or to dare proceeding directly toward the Void at the background of multiplicity, gradually preparing themselves, with the help of the elders, the gurus or teachers, already ahead on the same direction, to face that Void without succumbing to the fear of Its immensity. It is, in fact, human nature to be finite, therefore imperfect or ill at easy in existence. One of the ways to redress or compensate this 'finitude' is precisely to wrap it with the close association of other equally finite beings in need of reciprocal protection and security; the other is to accept the challenge of the cosmic vastness—or the Void or the Spirit beyond grasp and comprehension—by slowly approaching it through a suitable training involving a gradual letting go of all human attachments, thoughts and even self-awareness till realizing the ridiculously small seize of the ego. The next step in all spiritual disciplines is then the obvious renunciation to any pretence of inner identity, either by denying any ontological existence of its own or by so shifting the centre of one's concentration and awareness toward that Void, also conceivable as Fullness that only remains, either as Impersonal Absolute (the Brahman) or as a Personal All-embracing God. To this effect, as many gurus and holy people agree especially nowadays, the three traditional ways of the Spirit do not differ much in their final attainment. All of them, with a greater or lesser emphasis, end up by the final wiping out of the 'walking subject'. Practically, in fact, whether the elimination of the seeker is reached through an active presence in life but without desires for rewards or results, or through meditation aiming at a direct disappearance in the Absolute, or through the mystical embrace with the Divine so as to forget oneself, it is not a very relevant issue. There is no difference in the three attitudes as such; the difference is found only on their theoretical intellectual formulations and conceptualisations, which, as important as they may be, bear a less impact on the final liberation aimed at.

And here we can close by acknowledging a paradox: the individual, as such, is the ultimate subject of every experience, either clustered in social groups or striving toward a personal total realization. Yet, in both ways his very aim is his own elimination: either as an insignificant entity whose private aspirations have to be merged into the social, cultural and religious stream of the community he belongs to, or as an ontic or psychological nil who has no separate consistence before the all-pervading Supreme Divine.

CONCLUSIONS

At the end of this extremely compact presentation of the Cultural and Spiritual Heritage of Brahmanic India, one is obviously aware of the many shortcomings and quick generalizations unavoidable in such an extensive field of enquire. In a way, completeness was not in the scope itself of this research. The choice of any study involving such a fluid matter as human stand and behaviour is between dwellings on exactness in details——and in this case the subject matter has to be restrained within workable boundaries in a given space or a limited historical period——or to aim at a presentation of a whole picture, in which case the broadness of the panorama is responsible for lack of completeness and blurring of particular facts. Indian Dharma is like a well-cut Diamond, shining through endless facets but not allowing a simultaneous awareness of the shine as such proceeding from the entire precious stone and of every single cut considered in isolation. If you concentrate on the latter you loose the whole, and vice-versa if you admire the whole with the pure shining of its light you cannot perceive all the plans except for few landmarks catching the direct rays of a luminous source. Even such few ones may vary with changes of perspective and the position of the eye watching at it.

So it has been the case with this work: here, at the contrary of my previous book for which a somewhat broader picture of Vedic culture was reached through focussing on a specific ritualistic point, I choose to catch the light of a birth-view of a cultural, social, religious as well as spiritual panorama at the expenses of completeness in details. Many points have been overlooked altogether (like Tantrism, the various systems of philosophy or Dharsanas, the regional differences, especially important those of South moving somewhat on different lines and premises..., and also people living in a somewhat different nature, less exposed to the excesses of the North plains, like people of Bengal, Orissa, Gujarat and many others...), while others have been merely touched upon, (like festivals, in the philosophy behind sacred iconography, the counting of time,) each of whose could be worthy a monograph for itself. But this is not the main point. As the sub-title specifies, the idea behind this presentation is that of focussing on the spirit standing under the whole cultural and religious construction, elaborated by a people, or groups of a loosely related race, in the course of about 5.000 years or more. In working out this huge amount of data as mainly preserved in the Sacred Texts, beginning from the earlier Rgvedic hymns, down to the more recent Puranas, I was rather stricken by the possibility that the central axis of the whole Dharmic culture is to be found in the Yajurveda together with the (often despised or almost forgotten) Brahmanas. And this means that the main traits of this World-vision have being forged after setting into a sedentary and agricultural type of life. In the endless discussions of the Brahmanas referring, besides their own point of view in ritual matters, also to other contradictory proposals or solutions on difficult issues, is recorded the staggering effort of the Seers and the priests to reconsider, in the light of a changed manner of existence, the immense religious, cultic, and behavioural patrimony of a lost yet idealized past, where cattle were the main source of wealth and nomadic whereabouts in search of suitable pastures the normal mode of life. The past had to be brought into the present in need of unifying ritual patterns to deal with a changed geographical milieu on which to build again a workable cultural universe on which to fix and tame the future.

Since it is a commonly held opinion——though recently scholars seem to reconsider the issue——that in India there is a different conception of history than that hold by Westerners, I did not stress but vaguely an 'historical' sequence, though I tried to maintain a kind of order of precedence in overlapping of situations and growth of ideas. Any culture, also the most historically driven, has a tendency to consider itself in the position held in the *present moment*, so that its main feature is formed by decanting all the contributions brought about during the countless preceding ages, even if some have faded away because 'out of fashion'. In an all-comprehensive glance, all amounts to be a kind of struggle for better expressing the same existential predicaments, changing external attitudes only as far as it is felt necessary for better grasping Reality or for a better adaptation to It.

In what said up to now I wanted to stress the inner unitarian coherence of what appears to be a conglomerate of different Gods, world-views, attitudes, walks in life, and the like, that is to say of what generally strikes the outsider as a mass of paradoxes and contradicting points of views.

And one of these contradictions that can be eliminated is the wide-spread idea that Indian philosophy and spirituality despise this world, while experience shows that the majority of people are concretely struggling to better their allotted standard of life, and do not consider their efforts vested. The fact is that the two positions correspond to two different level of awareness: the world, with its cultural, social and religious rules and devises, is real, concrete and worthwhile for those who are merged in it; it reveals itself as deprived of substance only to those (and are a small minority) who had reached a degree of inner detachment. Like in a picture-hall, people emotionally driven may be carried away by the story projected on the screen; while more levelled spectators would watch it with cool detached appreciation. It is not indifference or lack of sensibility, but a hard conquered spiritual position, which does not prevent the sage to care for the people still involved in it, by helping them out of troubles with worldly advises and spiritual guide toward a liberation from it by presenting as many possible paths as suited to subjects coming from all levels of intellectual and social standards.

Perhaps, one of the reasons attracting Western youth to Indian ways of life and religious outlooks is the variety of paths displayed in front of them, in contrast with the monolithic tendency of Monotheistic Christianity. In India they find freedom combined with discipline and perpetually new perspectives as they advance in spiritual knowledge. The presence of qualified Masters entitled to interpret tradition according to the exigencies of the times and of their particular disciples is warrant for freedom and continuity in a fluid orthodox line which, in spite of some superficial discrepancies here and there, runs rather smoothly and without substantial interruptions from Vedic pre-history till now, ready to continuing steadily into the future, notwithstanding some gloomy but not commonly shared opinions to the contrary.

One can add here a warning against an easy 'positivistic' assumption that the traditional faith stored on the staggering role played by Rishis, or Realized persons at large, in the transmission and even forging of religious Truths is not due to a cryptic feeling of atheism——as could be the case for Western psychoanalysts——but to the recognition of their acquired unity with the Absolute. Through this unity, they acquired also "the authority and the power to mediate between the seeker and the supreme Object of seeking...and he can, if he so chooses...to break the seal of the seeker's consciousness..." because he "has transcended the limitations of the mental consciousness and had a direct access to superior modes of knowledge and action" (Kireet Joshi, The Veda and Indian Culture,

Rashtriya Veda Vidya Pratishthan, Delhi, 1991, p.41). And all along Indian history, such influence has been extended also to find out the above mentioned coordinates for interpreting, giving a meaning and bestowing an order to Reality, thus making life a liveable venture.

Another possible feeling that this presentation may not be free from the bias of positivistic detachment bordering to atheistic attitude is the high role given to geography as a decisive factor in moulding Indian cultural and religious expressions. To a mentality which, willy nilly, (even when it denies its assumptions) has been accustomed to the transcendental parameters imposed by Christianity, a bearing of geographical contingent reality on such vital issues as spiritual 'revelations' seems *ipso facto* to devaluate any conception of a Supreme Power which, for its very 'nature', should be untouched by and be above any petty earthly influence. Yet, even the highest transcendental Divine, if ever could be conceived at all had to 'come down' to the understandable level of Its human interpreters and mouthpieces: the Rishis, Shamans, seers, philosophers and theologians of all kind; and those intermediaries and builders of the various cultures and religious expressions cannot help to be influenced by what geographical conditions surround them. All religions grown with the people residing in specific areas——that is practically all those belonging to the many groups mentioned in the Foreword with the exception of the three belonging to the fourth and a few in the fifth——are bound to be exposed with images drawn from the immediate experience of the physical surroundings. And these, at their own turn, weight on people in such a way as to compel them to react to its stimuli either by adapting their own mode of life to it or by forcing it into more suitable cultural patterns through appropriate changes. In this respect, Indian geography in particular imposes itself with such a forceful evidence that dealing with it was not only an intellectual utilization of its suggestions as means of expressing Truths beyond verbalization, but was also a matter of sheer survival from its severe conditions. Therefore, the idea that the Brahmanic special character, somehow so peculiar to this country as to have become rather different from the other Indo-European groups migrated toward the West, is due, among other factors of course, to the special influence exercised on its elite by geographical conditions should not appear too far-fetched or foreign to the awareness of its own people.

MORE TITLES ON HINDUISM
FROM PILGRIMS PUBLISHING

www.pilgrimsbooks.com

For Catalog and more Information Mail or Fax to:

PILGRIMS BOOK HOUSE
Mail Order, P. O. Box 3872, Kathmandu, Nepal
Tel: 977-1-4700919 Fax: 977-1-4700943
E-mail: mailorder@pilgrims.wlink.com.np